The Unsolved
Mysteries
of the Bible

The Unsolved Mysteries of the Bible

Yohane

iUniverse LLC
Bloomington

THE UNSOLVED MYSTERIES OF THE BIBLE

iUniverse books may be ordered through booksellers or by contacting:

iUniverse LLC
1663 Liberty Drive
Bloomington, IN 47403
www.iuniverse.com
1-800-Authors (1-800-288-4677)

ISBN: 978-1-4917-0941-2 (sc)
ISBN: 978-1-4917-0943-6 (hc)
ISBN: 978-1-4917-0942-9 (e)

Library of Congress Control Number: 2013917750

Printed in the United States of America.

iUniverse rev. date: 10/03/2013

To the faithful

Contents

Introduction

Who am I?
Why am I here?
Who's in charge?
How can I be happy?

These questions may be considered the eternal wonders of mankind—the answers to which may be found in the Bible.

The Bible is a mysterious and oddly curious book. Given a different name, the Bible would be hard-pressed to find a publisher willing to overcome its many anomalies. For example:

1. Its lackluster title. Translated: "The Book."
2. No foreword or introduction.
3. No author biography (unknown).
4. No cited references to support its revelations.
5. No premise.
6. No bibliography.
7. Grammar and spelling—a challenge.
8. Organization and continuity issues.
9. Its content is often mysterious and confusing.
10. "Faith" is a prerequisite.

Despite these technical challenges, the Bible remains the most read book in the world according to Lit Couture: 3.9 billion (!) copies have been published and sold within the past fifty years. In a distant second place is *The Quotations from Chairman Mao Tse-Tung*, at 820 million copies.

The Bible's immense popularity could be due to "faith"—faith that God may be found in the Bible. Or, perhaps it is mankind's abiding wonder about his place in the Cosmos and the Bible's promise to provide the answers. However, because of its curious style, the Bible's "answers" appear cryptic rather than forthright. This may be one of the greater mysteries: the Bible does not attempt to persuade, convince, or prove—*it simply bestows*—suggesting a responsibility of the individual to "awaken spiritually" to receive the words of God.

An important aspect of *The Unsolved Mysteries of the Bible* is to establish a spiritual foundation from which the words of God may be perceived. Topics such as the nature and workings of God, evolution, reincarnation, angels, demons, the spiritual world, etc., are examined in relation to scripture and the laws of God. Therefore, combining intellectual knowledge with spiritual knowledge is encouraged. As an example, the creation of heaven and earth may be viewed as having occurred *only once*. It then follows that everything shares a common origin; that is, the origin of the world and of mankind is *one*. Thus, *everything that is committed is done unto itself*. Ergo, scripture's "As ye sow, so shall ye reap" and "Do unto others as you would have others do unto you."

The knowledge of the creation of heaven and earth served as the foundation for man's understanding of whom he is, why he is here, and the purpose for his being. This precious knowledge, along with its recorded history, was taken with man as he traveled and populated the earth, and it served as the cornerstone for the world's great civilizations.

Man, a child of God, preserved these precious records in his own languages on stone, clay tablets, scrolls, and metal plates. Because they documented man's relationship with his Creator, they were considered sacred; therefore, they were jealously guarded and preserved for posterity. Secreted away in temples, mosques, shrines, monasteries, and churches throughout the world may be found the ancient records of man in the form of religious texts, prophecies, world histories, mythologies, and oral traditions.

With the advent of modern science and technology, many of these records—such as the Dead Sea scrolls, Egyptian hieroglyphs, Mayan codices, Sumerian text, oral traditions, etc.—have been brought to light and translated. Researchers and scholars have found them to be strikingly similar (being of one origin), and they appear to support one another as parts of a grand mosaic that testify of the Fatherhood of God and the brotherhood of man.

Therefore, the Bible's greatness goes beyond the confines of religions. Being a part of the ancient record of man, it was transported from the Garden of Eden and protected and promulgated by many civilizations—the civilizations of the West bringing it forth into our modern era. Not being lost or hidden, the Bible is readily accessible to anyone who desires it, and—regarded as the most published book in the world—it offers the best opportunity for enlightenment and salvation for the greater good.

To solve the mysteries of the Bible will require accessing various sources of supporting data as well as information that may be considered divinely inspired; therefore, it is helpful to temporarily set aside preconceptions and view things with an open mind. In many instances, *The Unsolved Mysteries of the Bible* will be providing new information in an organized fashion that will allow resolving the many mysteries of the Bible at one's own comfort level.

Biblical references will be from the King James Version of the Bible (the Catholic Bible has been consulted as a cross-reference). Scientific data will be from many disciplines, especially the fields of physics, astrophysics, quantum mechanics, paleontology, parapsychology, archaeology, and the study of ancient religions and records.

The Unsolved Mysteries of the Bible has been organized by various topics, which allow immediate access to subjects of interest;

however, most topics prepare a foundation for the subjects that follow. Therefore, it is helpful to start at the beginning.

It is hoped that all will have a joyful and enlightening experience in their journey discovering the many mysteries of God and the Bible. In doing so, one may finally begin to see, feel, understand, and draw nigh to the God that has been longed for, deep within his or her heart.

Chapter 1

What Is the Bible?

The word "bible" is derived from the Greek *biblio*, which simply means "book." The Bible is indeed a collection of individual books such as the book of Genesis, the book of Psalms, the books of the New Testament, etc.

The Bible may be viewed as the ancient records of man that reveal the existence of a Creator God and a divine realm, how life and the universe came into being, the law by which all life flourishes, the relationship between God and humans, the purpose for the creation of humankind, records of the Earth's history, and information concerning God's divine plan. Such vital information has served as the foundation for all of the world's great civilizations and religions.

The ancient records were accorded various names as the ancient Hebrew, Israelite, Egyptian, Jewish, Greek, Roman, Eastern, and Western civilizations preserved them. "Bible" is the name used in our modern era, and it serves as the holy book for the Christian religion.

The Bible consists of two main divisions referred to as the "old" and "new" testaments. These terms were established by the Christian religion to designate the ancient records covering the period before the appearance of Jesus (the Old Testament) and the records relating to the period after Jesus's appearance (the New Testament). The Old Testament is also known as the *Tanach* of the Jewish religion. Hence, the Bible encompasses two world religions and is often referred to as being "Judeo-Christian." A key point of difference between Judaism and Christianity is that Christianity professes Jesus to be the promised Messiah prophesied in the Old Testament—therefore, the Bible consists of the Old and New Testaments. Judaism professes that the promised Messiah is yet to come—hence, its holy book does not include the New Testament.

However, the Bible is more than a collection of antiquated books of religion. The information contained within the Bible is universal in scope and is a heritage for all humankind, and if it may be received, the Bible is a record of one's own ancestors dating back hundreds of thousands of years. It truly is a rare gift.

Chapter 2
The Origin of the Bible

The Words of God

God bestowed "The Way of the Tree of Life" to humankind.

The Cherubim

God's first representatives on Earth—the cherubim of the
Garden of Eden—served as keepers and disseminators of the
Words of God (the ancient records).

The Ancient Hebrews

The Hebrews brought forth the ancient records
(the Old Testament).

The Egyptians

In the third century BC, the Greek Egyptian king, Ptolemy
II, commissioned seventy-two Jewish scholars to translate the
ancient records from Hebrew into Greek. Scholars refer to this
Greek translation as the Septuagint.

The Greeks

The Greeks translated and propagated the original Hebrew text of the ancient records—today referred to as the Old Testament of the Bible.

The Jews

The Jews created a Jewish version of the ancient records. This version did not include some of the text found in the original Greek Septuagint translation.

The Romans

Circa 325 AD, the Christian religion was formed with the pope serving as titular head in Rome. Catholicism used the original text of the Septuagint (Old Testament) and added the records of Jesus (New Testament) to form the Christian Bible.

The Europeans

In 1517 AD, Martin Luther and others protested against the excesses of Catholicism, resulting in the formation of the Protestant religion. This new religion adopted the Jewish version of the Old Testament and combined it with the New Testament to create a Protestant version of the Bible.

Many versions of the Bible are in use today, the essential difference being in the amount of Old Testament text each version contains. Some of these differing texts have been referred to as apocryphal (not part of doctrine), anagignoskomena (things that are read) and pseudepigrapha (apocryphal writings that do not appear in printed editions of the Bible). Also, new archaeological discoveries of the ancient records of man—such as the Dead Sea scrolls—are not part of the Bible, but they continue to expand man's knowledge of the Bible and ancient history.

The Bible's origin may be one of the true mysteries of the Bible itself. Scholars hold varying opinions concerning this issue. Moses is generally credited with authoring the first five books—Genesis, Exodus, Leviticus, Numbers, and Deuteronomy—of the Old Testament. It is probable that these and the other books of the Old Testament were derived from the ancient records maintained by the Cherubim of the Garden of Eden.

This thumbnail sketch represents an oversimplification of the Bible's complex and involved genesis. However, it serves to provide a sense of chronology and appreciation for the effort of the many civilizations that have made it possible to receive the Bible of today.

Chapter 3

Is the Bible the Word of God?

For many, the answer would be yes. For example, the revelation concerning how heaven, earth, and all the forms of life were created is information of which only its creator, or God, would have knowledge.

The Bible is also the work of man, who has diligently recorded God's words and the history of the world since the beginning of time. As a result, the Bible also reflects the imperfect words of man.

Thus, the perfect words of God have been recorded, preserved, translated, and promulgated by man to the best of his ability. However, a problem arises when there are differences of opinion concerning the *interpretation* of God's words. Such differences have resulted in the formation of divergent religions, denominations, and sects, and history demonstrates that the words of God have also been misused by the unscrupulous for personal gain and the control of others. This has caused doubt and confusion about God and the Bible, making the path to God unduly perilous, resulting in the loss of many lives.

Due to reasons related to God's divine plan, God and the Bible have been cloaked in mystery. However, scripture promises that at a future time—"In the last days, the house of the Lord shall be established in the top of the mountains and many nations shall flow into it and be taught of the ways of God" (Micah 4:1-2)—the mystery of God shall end.

The times and seasons indicate the appearance of such a wondrous time. Technology and the informational age have made it possible for science and religion to finally find common ground in which they may each contribute their knowledge to reveal the true living God—the God of science and religion.

Chapter 4

Is There Only One God?

The word *God* is not a name; rather, it is a term signifying the manifestation of divine power and spirit. Just as a man has a formal name, so does God (the Creator) have a formal name. However, God's formal name is not known on earth, nor is it ever spoken in heaven due to its extreme sacredness. Man has been allowed to refer to God by using words that describe various characteristics of God—words such as Yahweh, Jehovah, Father in heaven, Creator, etc. Thus, the word *god* (written in lowercase) may be considered a general term referring to a power other than man. As such, there are a multitude of gods (deities of divine power and spirit who are servants of God) that the Bible refers to as elders, lords, archangels, angels, etc. In Psalm 138:1, King David of Israel refers to these deities (gods) while singing praise to God: "I will praise thee with my whole heart: before the gods will I sing praise unto thee."

The concept of only "one God," or of *worshipping* only one God, originated with God's unique relationship with patriarchs Noah, Abraham, Isaac, and Jacob. They were instructed to serve and worship only the creator. In Genesis 14:22, Abraham professes his allegiance to God: "And Abram said to the king of Sodom, I have lift up mine hand unto the Lord, the most high God, the possessor of heaven and earth." In Mark 5:7, Jesus is referred to as "thou Son of the most high God," and in 1 Corinthians 8:5-6, Jesus's disciples expressed their knowledge of the divine hierarchy and their allegiance to God: "For though there be that are called gods, whether in heaven or in earth (as there be gods many, and lords many). But to us there is but one God, the Father, of whom are all things."

It may be understood that God (the Creator) is the power that creates and orchestrates everything in heaven and on earth. The servants of God (elders, lords, angels, etc.) are the deities (gods) who carry out God's will. Revelation 11:3-4 makes reference to two of God's witnesses, described as "two olive trees" and as "two candlesticks standing before the God of the earth." The "God of the earth" undoubtedly refers to a great god (elder) appointed to oversee the functioning of God's will in the physical realm (earth and the universe). "Standing before the God of the earth" indicates that the two servants (two candlesticks) of God were serving under the protection and jurisdiction of the god of the earth.

Thus, the Bible teaches that there are many "gods" (deities who are worthy to serve God in heaven or on earth) but that there is only one God that should be worshipped—that is, "the most high God," and "the Father of whom are all things" (1 Corinthians 8:5-6). Although the Bible demonstrates that the servants of God were often treated with great respect, the Bible clearly discerns the difference between "respecting" and "worshipping." Jesus was very strict concerning this point. In Matthew 19:17, Jesus admonished a follower by saying, "Why callest me good? There is none good but one, that is, God."

These verses reveal that the servants of God thoroughly understood the divine order of God's kingdom—God being the most high god and the only one that should be praised and worshipped. Even the holy one, Jesus, was very strict in maintaining this order. Likewise, the faithful should follow the example of their master and praise and worship only God—the Father of all things. Doing so would be the important *first step* on the path that leads to oneness with the true, living God.

Chapter 5

Is God a Jealous and Vengeful God?

Verses in scripture characterize God as jealous and vengeful. In the Old Testament's Nahum 1:2, Nahum the Elkoshite records in a vision, "God is jealous, and the Lord revengeth; the Lord revengeth, and is furious; the Lord will take vengeance on his adversaries, and he reserveth wrath for his enemies."

Similarly, in Exodus 20:5-7: "For I the Lord thy God am a jealous God, visiting the iniquity of the fathers upon the children unto the third and fourth generation of them that hate me." And, in Genesis 6:11-13: "The earth also was corrupt before God, and the earth was filled with violence. And God looked upon the earth, and, behold, it was corrupt; for all flesh had corrupted his way upon the earth. And God said unto Noah, The end of all flesh is come before me; for the earth is filled with violence through them; and, behold, I will destroy them with the earth."

These earlier, stern characterizations of God appear in stark contrast with the modern understanding that God is love and that we are all children of God. When viewed over the vast expanse of time that the Bible encompasses, could these characterizations of God be interpreted as God revealing more about himself? That is, God is not only strictness but also love?

It has been said, "An apple does not fall very far from the tree." As children of God, we need not look far from ourselves to have a sense of what God may be like. As an example, we all have a sense of justice and fair play. Most parents would immediately correct unfairness between siblings either verbally, by employing restrictions, or with the use of corporal punishment—and doing so, without much wonder where such wisdom comes from. Could the sense of justice and fairness and holding sway over it be divine characteristics inherited from God? And it goes without saying that the correcting parent would be considered biased and possibly even "vengeful" by the one being corrected—and the same parent would be considered fair and righteous by the one who had been wronged.

It is interesting that "strictness" has often been referred to in modern parlance as "tough love." This may be indicative of just how permissive and uncaring modern culture has become, and it appears to be reflected by today's frivolous youth.

It would be safe to say that God possesses the wisdom not to be a doting or permissive parent that spoils his children. God exercises strictness and mercy commensurate to the needs of the individual. This—the essence of true love—reflects God's nature and close relationship with his children.

Chapter 6

What Is God?

The essence of God is "power"—the power to create, materialize, and maintain everything that is in the universe. God is the only power that exists. Everything else borrows from God's power. "Power" transcends religion and science. Power (God) exists whether one believes in it or not, or whether it is perceivable or not.

God's power manifests on earth as, for example, the forces of gravity, magnetism, and electricity. (It is curious that science, not able to fully explain how these forces function, considers them to be largely a mystery; likewise, religion considers God to be equally mysterious.) Each of these forces is fundamental to the existence and functioning of all matter from the microcosm of subatomic particles to the macrocosm of the universe. Without these powers or forces, everything as we know it would revert to the primordial mass before heaven and earth was created. It may be said that "existence," all that is, is the *physical and spiritual* manifestation of God. Therefore, God is everything and everywhere. This understanding about God has served as an aspect of worship through the veneration of nature and all life-forms by the Hindu and Buddhist religions, as examples.

Interestingly, the study of "power" has been discretely relegated to the realm of scientific inquiry, where God is not acknowledged. In reality, this is an area where science and religion may enlarge mankind's understanding about God. For example, science quantifies "power" as something impersonal and measurable. Religion quantifies "power" as conscious and communicable. Together, both views provide a clearer understanding about the mystery of God (e.g., proof that God exists).

God is also "totality," which encompasses everything: God is both strictness and mercy, both positive and negative, both vertical and horizontal (combined as +), both personal (our Creator) and impersonal (nature), both male (Father in heaven) and female (Mother Nature), both omnipresent (the universe) and present (as God), both omnipotent (the awesome power of the universe) and potent (limited power, bestowing "free will" and allowing man to serve as his magistrate on earth).

Although God manifests as the perfect balance of both positive and negative aspects of creation, the Bible reveals that God places priority on the positive, male, spiritual aspects and ascribes a subordinate role on the negative, female, material aspects of creation. As examples, God manifested as Father in heaven; the scepter of God was passed down through the patriarchs Noah, Abraham, Isaac, and Jacob; Eve served as a subordinate/helpmate to Adam; and humankind is directed to lay up treasures in heaven rather than on earth. The principle of separate and equal with priority placed on one helps to more clearly define the functioning of God's will. In practical terms, this principle may be understood as living one's life by combining "the way of the world" with "the way of God," with priority placed on the way of God (following commandments, etc.). Living in such a manner is to live life on earth in the realm where good health, harmony, and prosperity abound.

The concept of power/consciousness has been expanded by various scientific studies. The science of particle physics (e.g., Nobel laureate Dr. Hideki Yukawa, discoverer of the meson) has determined that space is not a "vacuum," but rather is filled with high-energy particles that constantly rain down upon the earth, continually generating and maintaining life. It could be said that this life-giving and life-sustaining power or energy, which permeates the macrocosm of the universe and the microcosm of the atom, is the manifestation of God's love, wisdom, and will.

In 1939, Russian researcher Semyon Kirlian discovered a photographic technique, called Kirlian photography, that suggested physical evidence for the existence of energy fields. Kirlian images rendered energy fields (aura, life force, spiritual power, etc.) as varying, multicolored electrical emanations that surround all animate and inanimate objects that appear to be influenced by human emotions. This invisible power or energy field may be termed "consciousness." Thus, communication through mental telepathy—such as intention or prayer—is an ever-present reality.

Kirlian photographs also suggest that power/consciousness exists in plants. A March 3, 2005, article, "New Research Opens a Window on the Minds of Plants," by Patrik Jonsson, staff writer for the *Christian Science Monitor,* confirms that plants have the ability to acquire and apply knowledge, and they have the power of self-recognition. Researchers concede that a big part of intelligence is self-consciousness and that plants do have that.

The interest in plant intelligence/consciousness is gaining worldwide interest. An October 30, 2007, *Wired Magazine* article by Nicole Martinelli reported on the establishment of the International Laboratory of Plant Neurobiology, located near Florence, Italy. Headed by Professor Stefano Mancuso, a teacher of horticulture at the University of Florence, the laboratory is the only one of its kind dedicated to the study of plant intelligence. Their research has revealed that plants have the remarkable capacity to solve problems and determine the best way to grow, adapt, and thrive. Professor Mancuso believes that if intelligence is defined as the capacity to solve problems, then plants have a lot to teach us—without human neurosis.

Experiments using galvanometers ("lie detectors") to measure the electrical field/consciousness of plants have shown that plants also have the ability to sense the thoughts of humans and respond accordingly. When researchers projected violent thoughts to plants, the instruments attached to them recorded extremely agitated reactions, while positive, nurturing thoughts elicited very calm responses. These tests proved what plant lovers the world over, without test equipment, have known all along: plants respond to love.

At what level of consciousness would animals be placed? Those who love animals already know the answer. Animals require kindness and dignity similar to humans because they share the same life force that emanates from God—the important difference is that humans serve as God's magistrate on earth, and animals serve to make the earth habitable by maintaining balance in nature.

Do inanimate objects possess "consciousness"? This is an intriguing question that is yet to be resolved. Perhaps the presence of the pulsating and vibrating energy field surrounding such objects suggests the affirmative—albeit perhaps "consciousness" in a different form or level than may be understood. The phenomenon of "mind over matter" and the power of positive thinking add to the mystery.

With the incredible advances being made in science—the essence of matter has been identified as vibrating loops of energy—it appears that science is bridging the gap that separates the physical and spiritual worlds. In this regard, science is finally beginning to grasp what religion has accepted on faith; that is, the physical realm is but a manifestation of the truly existing, unseen realm of spirit.

It is probable that technology will soon make it possible to communicate with the spiritual world (voices and images of the deceased are already being recorded and photographed). It is hoped that as technology and man's spiritual level rise, direct communication—as is presently made possible by telecommunication—may be accomplished with the higher levels of the spiritual world: the realm of angels, archangels, elders, and, ultimately, God.

Chapter 7

The Divine Science
of Creation

Genesis 1:1-3: "In the beginning, the earth was without form, and void; and darkness was upon the face of the deep. And the spirit of God moved upon the face of the waters." The "spirit of God *moved* upon the face of the waters" symbolizes the manifestation of the concept of *space*. "And God said, Let there be light: and there was light." "Let there be light" symbolizes the manifestation of God's power as light and consciousness.

Genesis 1:4-5: "And God saw the light, that it was good: and God divided the light from the darkness. And God called the light Day, and the darkness he called Night. And the evening and the morning were the first day." From God were generated the two primary forces of creation as represented by "day" (+) and "night" (–). "And the evening and the morning were the first day," symbolizes the manifestation of the concept of *time*.

Genesis 1:6-8: "And God said let there be a firmament in the midst of the waters, and let it divide the waters from the waters . . . And God called the firmament Heaven. And the evening and the morning were the second day." The firmament, Heaven, symbolizes the creation of the divine spiritual realm.

Genesis 1:9-10: "And God said, Let the waters under the heaven be gathered together unto one place, and let the dry land appear . . . And God called the dry land Earth." "Earth" symbolizes the creation of the physical realm.

Genesis 1:11-12: "And God said, Let the earth bring forth grass, the herb yielding seed, and the fruit tree yielding fruit after his kind . . . And the earth brought forth grass, and herb yielding seed after his kind, and the tree yielding fruit, whose seed was in itself, after his kind . . . And the evening and the morning were the third day." "Earth bring forth" what God created symbolizes the role of Mother Nature as being the hand of God working in the physical world. "Grass, herb, and fruit tree" indicates that the plant kingdom was the first form of life on earth.

Genesis 1:14: "And God said, Let there be lights in the firmament of the heaven to divide the day from the night; and let them be for signs, and for seasons, and for days, and years." "Lights in the firmament of heaven" refers to the creation of a divine hierarchy—elders, lords, archangels, angels, etc.—that fulfilled God's command to materialize time as discrete elements. "Let them be for signs, and for seasons, and for days, and years," indicates that the elements of time are synonymous with deities in the firmament of heaven.

Genesis 1:16-19: "And God made two great lights; the greater light to rule the day, and the lesser light to rule the night: he made stars also . . . And the evening and the morning were the forth day." "Two great lights" refers to the two great powers/deities (elders) that were generated from God to be responsible for the "day" (heaven) and the "night" (earth). "Greater light" and "lesser light" designates rank and priority—the spiritual realm (greater light) being of main importance, and the physical realm (lesser light) being subordinate. The creation of stars refers to the materialization of the galactic heavens.

Genesis 1:20-23: "And God said, Let the waters bring forth abundantly the moving creature that hath life, and fowl that may fly above the earth . . . And God created great whales, and every living creature that moveth, which the waters brought forth abundantly, after their kind . . . And God blessed them, saying, Be fruitful and multiply, and fill the waters in the seas, and let fowl multiply in the earth. And the evening and morning were the fifth day." "Waters brought forth" reveals that Mother Nature materialized that for which God first created the spiritual pattern. "Moving creature" indicates that the animal kingdom was the second form of life to appear on earth.

Genesis 1:26: "And God said, Let us make man in our image, after our likeness: and let them have dominion over all the earth, and over every creeping thing that creepeth upon the earth." "Let us" refers to God and his divine hierarchy. "Make man in our image, after our likeness" indicates that man's spirit was patterned after that of his Creator. Thus, in all of God's creation, only man is considered to be the child of God.

Genesis 1:27-28: "So God created man in his own image, in the image of God created he him; male and female created he them. And God blessed them, and God said unto them, Be fruitful, and multiply, and replenish the earth, and subdue it: and have dominion over the fish of the sea, and over the fowl of the air, and over every living thing that moveth upon the earth." "In the image of God created he him; male and female created he them" indicates that human beings are the manifestation of the two basic aspects (+ and –) of God, and they are in the image of God. "Be fruitful, and multiply, and replenish the earth, and subdue it: and have dominion" indicates that man's purpose is to serve as a magistrate of God (i.e., man has been given the mission to rule the earth in God's absence or, specifically, to re-create a model of heaven on the earth). This verse reveals the inherent purpose for the creation of human beings.

Genesis 1:29-31: "And God said, Behold, I have given you every herb bearing seed, which is upon the face of all the earth, and every tree, in the which is the fruit of a tree yielding seed; to you it shall be for meat. And to every beast of the earth, and to every fowl of the air, and to every thing that creepeth upon the earth, wherein there is life, I have given every green herb for meat: and it was so. And God saw every thing that he had made, and, behold, it was very good. And the evening and the morning were the sixth day." These verses indicate that, in the beginning, God arranged that all life on earth would receive sustenance from the plant kingdom. Everything would exist in harmony, and there would be no taking of life of any kind.

Genesis 2:1-4: "Thus the heavens and the earth were finished, and all the host of them. And on the seventh day God ended his work that he had made; and he rested on the seventh day . . . These are the generations of the heavens and of the earth when they were created, in the day that the Lord God made the earth and the heavens." The term "generations" provides a better sense of the source and time in which heaven and earth were created. The latest scientific estimations indicate that the universe was created approximately eighteen billion years ago.

Throughout the process of the creation of heaven and earth, it is evident that God created the spiritual form for everything and commanded others (the earth/Mother Nature) to bring forth or materialize what he created. It can be seen that God did not work alone. At the start of creation, the primary powers (deities) of space, time, fire (+), and water (–) were generated from God. From these great powers, God generated the divine hierarchy, the rest of creation and finally humankind—over a period of billions of years. When one views the beauty of the earth and vastness of its heaven, one can't help but be awed by the unimaginable effort it must have taken to create such wonders; and one can realize the importance of doing the utmost to protect it.

The Creation of the Universe

1. God manifests as "light":

2. God generates the four powers of space, time, fire (+), and water (–) that form the foundation of the universe:

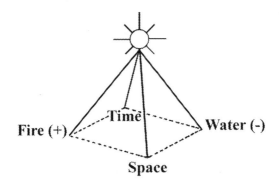

3. God creates the divine realm (heaven) followed by the physical realm (earth):

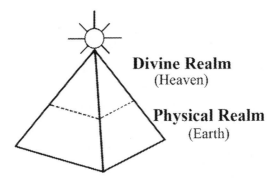

4. The astral realm was created when Adam and Eve were cast from the Garden of Eden:

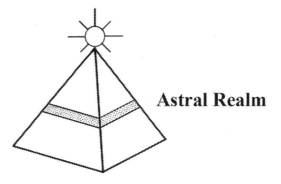

5. The pyramid symbolizes the "throne of God" and was the origin of *Sun* (God) *worship* (monotheism):

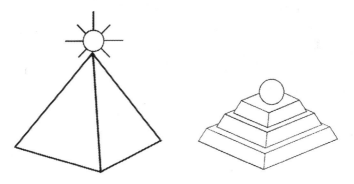

The ancient Hebrews and Israelites were the Sun (Creator God) worshippers and pyramid (God's holy altar) builders of earth's history. The Bible's patriarchs—Noah, Abraham, Isaac, and Jacob—all constructed holy altars (pyramids) to honor God. Genesis 8:20: "And Noah builded an altar unto the Lord; and took of every clean beast, and of every clean fowl, and offered burnt offerings on the altar." Genesis 12:7: "And the lord appeared unto Abram, and said, Unto thy seed will I give this land: and there builded he an altar unto the Lord, who appeared unto him." Genesis 26:23-25: "And he went up from thence to Beer-sheba. And the Lord appeared unto him the same night, and said, I am the God of Abraham thy father: fear not, for I am with thee, and will bless thee, and multiply thy seed for my servant Abraham's sake. And he builded an altar there, and called upon the name of the Lord, and pitched his tent there: and there Isaac's servants digged a well." Genesis 28:18, 22: "And Jacob rose up early in the morning, and took the stone that he had put for his pillows, and set it up for a pillar, and poured oil upon the top of it." *"And this stone, which I have set for a pillar, shall be God's house:* and of all that thou shalt give me I will surely give the tenth unto thee." Thus, the ancient Hebrews and Israelites were the pyramid builders of earth's ancient past. Where pyramids may be found today are the lands that God had granted to the ancient Hebrews and Israelites.

The book of Genesis reveals that mankind departed the Garden of Eden in the east and migrated to other parts of the world. Researchers have documented the existence of ancient pyramidal structures around the world, many predating the pyramids of Egypt. The oldest pyramids are found to be those existing in regions of Japan, China, and North and South America. These oldest pyramids coincide with the Bible's chronology for the establishment of the (earlier) ancient Hebrew and (later) Israelite civilizations.

The pyramid is an integral part of the seal of God's relationship with the patriarchs. The pyramid—with apex at top—symbolizes God bestowing from heaven. The inverted pyramid—with apex at bottom—symbolizes mankind worshipping God. These two pyramids, when *interlocked*—forming a six-pointed star hexagram—represent the covenant relationship between God and humankind. Therefore, this symbol may be found among many of the world's ancient religions, and—as the Star of David—it was associated with the Bible's Moses, King David, and Jesus.

Scripture reveals that the pyramid's origin dates back to antiquity and that the children of God built them to worship and honor God. Of equal importance is that the pyramid was constructed to withstand the passage of time to serve as a remnant to help unlock the mysteries of the Bible.

Chapter 8

Evolution

The American College Dictionary defines evolution as, "Any process of formation or growth or development." Hence, the essence of evolution is the process in which things occur gradually. The opposite of evolution is revolution. Revolution is defined as, "A complete or marked change in something." The essence of revolution is the process when things occur rapidly. Both evolution and revolution are observable in life, which indicates that God uses both processes to accomplish and maintain his creation.

Evolution, when change occurs slowly, is the usual way in which life functions. It can be seen in the gradual way that night turns into day, in the gradual way that a baby grows into an adult, and in the gradual changing of the seasons.

Evolution, a principle of step-by-step change, is one of the laws that God established at the time of creation to maintain harmony and order. It is a reflection of God's will. Evolution is also an arrangement by God to allow mankind to gradually attain perfection of the soul to become Christlike. Just as parents patiently nurture their children to become successful adults, so does God patiently nurture his children to become children of God. "To patiently nurture" is possible due to the principle of step-by-step change, or evolution.

In the book of Genesis, chapter 1, God commanded the earth and waters to bring forth abundantly what God created. Thus, all life materialized on earth through the effort of Mother Nature.

God created the *spiritual pattern*, and nature developed the physical form or body for what God had created. Science is beginning to discover the incredible way in which life was created and how life adapts to survive in ever-changing environments. The ability to adapt over long periods of time results in subtle changes within species. These changes are explained as the work of evolution. However, science has yet to record one species changing or evolving into another, as exemplified by its search for a "missing link." This is so because each life-form is unique unto itself, having been created with a distinct spiritual pattern.

Science reveals that all life is made up of the basic elements—carbon, hydrogen, oxygen, nitrogen, etc. The invisible power that arranges these basic elements to form an animal, vegetable, or mineral is the spiritual pattern created by God. Thus, a cow can never *naturally evolve* into a horse, or a cat into a dog, or an ape into a man.

Science and religion appear to be counterparts or soul mates. There will be times when religion will have the clearer perspective (e.g., Man was created by God and did not evolve from the ape). And, there will be other times when science will have the better understanding (e.g., Creation did not occur in seven days, but rather over a period of billions of years). Therefore, it would appear that it is God's intent that religion and science should work together—each contributing its unique abilities—to successfully fathom the mysteries of God.

Note the spiritual pattern of an organism—created by the infinite and perfect wisdom of God—manifests on earth as something akin to what science identifies as the genetic code.

Chapter 9

God and Nature

Nature is the manifestation of God's power in the physical world. The awesome power of nature is the awesome power of God. It can be said that God is nature and nature is God. What is observable in nature are the physical workings of God. The awesome power of nature functioning is the invisible hand of God working to maintain purity and balance in his creation.

The word "natural" is derived from nature. "Natural" may apply to anything that has been created by God. In this context, "unnatural" may mean anything that has been manufactured by man. Our modern way of living, which focuses on technology, convenience, and the pursuit of material wealth, creates a highly "unnatural" environment, so one may unknowingly become distant from God simply by living in the modern way of life.

There is also natural food (food as God naturally provides), and there is unnatural food (food produced and processed by man). The difference is that what God has provided "naturally" is pure and perfect for the proper maintenance of the spirit, mind, and body; what man has produced is often, out of necessity, shown to contain unnatural agricultural chemicals, pesticides, growth hormones, antibiotics, preservatives, and other additives (many causing cancer and birth defects), which accumulate and contaminate the human body (the temple for the soul).

A Scripps Howard News Service article by Joan Lowy reported on the first nationwide attempt to measure pollution in people's bodies by the Center for Disease Control and Prevention. The 1999 CDC findings indicated surprisingly high levels of toxic chemicals in blood and urine samples of thirty-eight hundred people tested. Ms. Lowy's article also reported that many health experts believe that exposure to man-made chemicals may be linked to the increasing occurrence of cancer, tumors, Parkinson's disease, autism, genetic defects, and other chronic diseases.

The Bible reveals that what one consumes is of such importance that God gave specific guidance on this matter. Throughout chapter 11 of the book of Leviticus, God gave strict instructions to Moses and Aaron saying, "Speak unto the children of Israel, saying, These are the beasts which ye shall eat among all the beasts that are on the earth. Whatsoever parteth the hoof, and is cloven-footed, and cheweth the cud, among the beasts, that shall ye eat. Nevertheless these shall ye not eat of them that chew the cud, or of them that divide the hoof: as the camel . . . the coney . . . the hare . . . the swine . . . Of their flesh shall ye not eat, and their carcase shall ye not touch; they are unclean to you." God continued throughout the chapter by describing what should and should not be eaten of those animals that live in the waters, that fly in the air, and that crawl on the ground.

The key point in God's guidance concerning food is revealed in verse 44: "For I am the Lord your God; ye shall therefore sanctify yourselves, and ye shall be holy; for I am holy: neither shall ye defile yourselves with any manner of creeping thing that creepeth upon the earth." That is, eating what God has determined to be "unclean" defiles one's spirituality, *causing one to become unholy.* This appears to establish a link between diet and spirituality: It may be extrapolated that natural food (as God provides) nurtures spiritual development and oneness with God. Unnatural food (as manufactured by man) deters spiritual development, leading to separation from God. Separation from the true, living God—the creator of heaven and earth—leads to disease, poverty, and conflict.

The book of Daniel, chapter 1, illustrates the relationship between diet and spirituality. King Nebuchadnezzar, who wished to learn from the wisdom and science of the Israelites, sequestered the prophet Daniel and three others. To prepare Daniel and his companions to be fit to stand before the king, they were provided with the king's meat and wine for a period of three years. However, Daniel, being knowledgeable of the ways of God, beseeched his captor to be fed "pulse [peas, beans, lentils] and water" for a period of ten days, after which a comparison would be made with those being fed the king's meat and wine. The results were explained in Daniel 1:15, 17: "And at the end of the ten days their countenances appeared fairer and fatter in flesh than all the children which did eat the portion of the king's meat. As for these four children, God gave them knowledge and skill in all learning and wisdom: and Daniel had understanding in all visions and dreams." Daniel, who had "understanding in all visions and dreams" (Daniel had great spirituality), chose a vegetarian way of life (peas, beans, lentils). This appears to also be revealed for the Patriarch Jacob (father of the twelve tribes of Israel) as indicated in Genesis 25:29-34, "And Jacob sod pottage [a thick soup of lentils and bread]." Thus, scripture indicates that what one chooses to eat directly affects one's spirituality and the quality of one's relationship with God.

If the book of Leviticus was written today, would we receive similar guidance concerning the food of this modern age? Science has warned about the many carcinogens that may be found in the food that we eat. We now live in an age of strife, in which society, the family unit, and our educational system are stressed, and the human body is succumbing to all manner of disease. Is this "unholy" condition partly the result of being "defiled" by "unclean" food and water?

Many people are taking science's message to heart and are turning to food that God provides naturally. This would be food that has been grown "organically" without the use of agricultural chemicals and food additives, and without genetic modification.

GMO (genetically modified organism) is the process by which mankind's science—to provide for man's material needs—changes the genetic structure of a plant or animal for the sake of greater food production or greater resistance to disease. However, by tampering with an organism's genetic code, the perfection of what God has created is corrupted and rendered imperfect by man's science, mostly for reasons of economic expediency. In today's modern age of materialism, the pursuit of profit and wealth has become a prime objective, while the earth, nature, and people receive less consideration.

It is reasonable to assume that genetically modified organisms are not of God. GMOs may appear similar in appearance to what God has created. However, when an organism's spiritual pattern, as reflected by its genetic structure, has been modified, it has—by definition—been transformed into something that is out of step with nature. Can such a stranger to nature provide the necessary nourishment for man's spirit, mind, and body?

Insects seem to know the answer. Insects will shun GMO crops—such as corn—and will only feed on natural organisms produced by nature. A local non-GMO farmer explained why his corn was sold with its tops trimmed off: "It's because the tops are where the caterpillars live, so they must be removed when the corn is brought to market. However, commercially grown GMO corn is sold whole because insects will not feed on them."

It is curious how the lowly insect should be blessed with wisdom to discern what is edible while modern man, endowed with rational thought, should be lacking in this vital area. Perhaps this is a testament on the extent to which modern man has strayed from nature and God. Food that has been genetically modified is an important area in which caution should be exercised.

Nonprofit organizations, such as the Institute For Responsible Technology, are good sources of information on the topic of GMOs. Many concerned citizens have also become "label readers" and avoid products that contain unnatural, toxic substances that threaten the sanctity of the spirit, mind, and body.

A book that documents how food and medicine are affecting one's health is *The Hundred-Year Lie*, by Randall Fitzgerald. The author cautions succinctly how we are surrounded in an invisible sea of synthetic chemicals that our bodies absorb to toxic levels, to which the effects are treated with more synthetic drug compounds that often prove even more toxic to us, and this cycle repeats itself over and over.

The following are verses from the Bible concerning diet and longevity. Genesis 1:29: "And God said, Behold, I have given you every herb bearing seed, which is upon the face of all the earth, and every tree, in which is the fruit of a tree yielding seed; to you it shall be for meat." Genesis 1:30: "And to every beast of the earth, and to every fowl of the air, and to every thing that creepeth upon the earth, wherein there is life, I have given every green herb for meat." Genesis 5:5: "And all the days that Adam lived were nine hundred and thirty years."

These verses reveal that the great architect, God, arranged that the plant kingdom served as food and nourishment for all life on earth. Following this arrangement, man lived to nearly a thousand years of age. However, since then, man's eating habits have gradually changed along with a diminished lifespan that presently is about one hundred years of age. It may be safely concluded that better health and spiritual growth may be found by returning to what God naturally provides. Reflecting this realization, science recommends the addition of larger amounts of fresh fruits and vegetables into the modern diet to promote health and longevity.

It may be observed that when the body needs water, there is thirst. When the body needs food, there is hunger. When the body needs specific nutrients, there is craving for animal, vegetable, or mineral-bearing foods. God has arranged this simple mechanism in all creatures to perpetuate health and longevity; therefore, it is wise to follow nature. However, due to unnatural food addictions, it is also wise to be knowledgeable and avoid food that has been altered or which science has determined to be detrimental to good health.

In conclusion, it can be seen that the true, living God—manifesting as both Father in heaven and Mother Nature—has revealed the importance for properly maintaining the physical body due to its positive and negative influence on one's soul and spirit.

Research on calorie restriction and longevity conducted on rhesus monkeys, reported in the *New York Times,* July 10, 2009, revealed that animals fed thirty percent less food exhibited better overall health and longevity (better physical appearance, vitality, less disease) than their counterparts who were allowed to eat a full diet. It appears that less food results in less stress on the body, which is vital for good health. A healthy body has a positive influence on the mind and, ultimately, on the spirit.

The Japanese follow a dietary practice called "Hara hachi bu"—to eat eighty percent full. This simple practice, in conjunction with a natural diet, is believed responsible for making the people of Okinawa the longest-lived people on earth. A Japanese proverb goes something like this: "Eight parts of a full stomach sustain the man; the other two sustain the doctor."

It is good to combine God's scriptural guidance (to achieve holiness) with the latest findings in science (to achieve health). These may be considered components that are necessary to progress in becoming Christlike. It is difficult to progress when one is incapacitated by cancer, arthritis, diabetes, obesity, heart disease, kidney disease, depression, emphysema, and addictions to drugs and alcohol, etc. Maintaining good health is an expression of gratitude to God, and it is essential in all aspects of life.

Chapter 10

Reincarnation

Reincarnation is generally understood to mean the process by which a soul is born on earth more than once. The following is an example of how reincarnation may work: a soul departs from its home in the spiritual world and appears on earth as a newborn baby for the purpose of fulfilling God's will. Due to human limitations, the soul may not be able to attain perfection (become Christlike) in its lifetime, and it returns to the spiritual world to reflect on its life experience. After a period of reflection, the soul is allowed to reincarnate—that is, it is given another opportunity at life on earth to become Christlike. Through such an arrangement by God, a soul is allowed many opportunities to finally attain divinity and eternal life in heaven.

Besides the opportunity to attain perfection, a soul returning to earth is also presented with the opportunity to atone for sins that may have been committed, by experiencing the same for itself. This is the function of the law "as ye sow, so shall ye reap"/"do unto others as you would have others do unto you." This principle or law is referred to in Numbers 14:18, "The Lord is longsuffering, and of great mercy, forgiving iniquity and transgression, and by no means clearing the guilty, visiting the iniquity of the fathers upon the children unto the third and fourth generation." That is, after a period of three or four generations in the spiritual world, a soul ("the fathers") returns to earth as a newborn ("the children"), at which time it is allowed to atone for any sins that may have been committed. In popular terminology, "the iniquity of the fathers" is often referred to as "the baggage" each of us brings with us in life. The three and four generation time period between a soul's earthly appearances is for the purpose of "healing old wounds" so a soul may resume anew in the quest to become Christlike.

A curious arrangement by God is that souls are not allowed memories of their past lives. Perhaps memories are "egocentric" and are stumbling blocks in a soul's progress to grow spiritually. However, abilities such as skills and talents do remain with a soul and are brought forth to be developed further. Perhaps this arrangement is so because skills and talents are "pure" and untainted by the ego. Thus, all of the world's great entertainers, athletes, artists, musicians, scientists, statesmen, industrialists, financiers, inventors, etc., etc., etc., are said to have been "born that way." In truth, their talents and abilities are the result of pursuing their passion over many lifetimes, often through blood, sweat, and tears.

Several New Testament passages concerning Jesus and his disciples indicate that souls do appear on earth more than once. In John 16:28, Jesus reveals that he has appeared on earth before: "I came forth from the father, and am come into the world: again, I leave the world, and go to the Father." When Jesus said, "again, I leave the world," he was indicating that he had been born into the world before, having been sent by God, and that he was again returning to God.

In Micah 5:2, God speaks of the many earthly appearances of his servant Jesus: "But thou, Bethlehem Ephratah, though thou be little among the thousands of Judah, yet out of thee shall he come forth unto me that is to be ruler in Israel; whose goings forth have been from of old, from everlasting." "Whose goings forth" refers to Jesus's many departures from heaven to be born (Son of man) in the world as God's anointed. "From of old, from everlasting" is a reference to Jesus being the "alpha and omega"; that is, he has been appearing on earth since the beginning of time and will appear in the end as the "promised Messiah." In John 14:3, Jesus reveals that his disciples will also appear (reincarnate) with him at the time of his Second Coming: "I will come again, and receive you unto myself; that where I am, there ye may be also."

A compelling reason for God's anointed to appear as a human being (Son of man), is that most human beings cannot see into or communicate with the spiritual world. Thus, God sends his anointed to be born on earth to convey the words of God, and it appears that God has arranged for the disciples to be there to assist God's anointed.

Revelation 3:12 states that all humans experience many lifetimes on earth for the purpose of overcoming their human imperfections: "Him that overcometh will I make a pillar in the temple of my God, and he shall go no more out." "Go no more out" refers to someone no longer needing to leave the spiritual world to live another earthly life (reincarnate) because they have finally "overcometh" their human imperfections and have gained eternal life in heaven.

In Matthew 5:48, Jesus instructed his disciples, "Be ye therefore perfect, even as your Father which is in heaven is perfect." That is, humankind must overcome imperfections and shortcomings to be allowed to reside eternally with God. The principle of reincarnation may be viewed as God's arrangement that provides individuals with the opportunity to achieve perfection at their own rate.

The science of parapsychology has studied the phenomenon of reincarnation through many documented accounts of people's "past life" experiences. In these experiences, people have been able to recall previous lifetimes with names, places, things, and events that researchers have been able to confirm as existing and true.

Studies by researchers Dolores Cannon, Dr. Bruce Goldberg, Dr. Raymond Moody, Dr. Walter Semkiw, et al., reveal that many souls are now being reborn much sooner than "the third and fourth generation" between lifetimes on earth. The short time period between lifetimes makes it now possible to confirm one life with the records of a previous life.

An excellent account of a reincarnation experience was presented on *ABC News Prime Time Mysteries of the Paranormal*: "Was Boy a WWII Fighter Pilot?" The story, which aired on April 15, 2004, was about a child named James Leininger, who had an unusual love and knowledge of military aircraft. At the age of two years old, little James began to have frequent nightmares about being trapped in a burning, crashed airplane. His parents went though trying times attempting to make sense of it all, and it was James's grandmother who was first to suggest that perhaps James was reliving experiences of a past life.

As James grew older and was able to articulate about his dreams, he began to reveal startling details about the life of a former fighter pilot that had been shot down in the battle for Iwo Jima. James was also able to name the *Natoma* as the aircraft carrier from which he flew as well as give the names of fellow pilots.

James's father began searching the Internet, combing through military records and interviewing men who served aboard the *Natoma Bay*. His research revealed that only one aircraft from the *Natoma Bay* was lost during the battle for Iwo Jima on March 3, 1945, and the pilot's name was James M. Houston Jr. Testimonies of other pilots who participated in the battle also confirmed the details of information revealed in little James Leininger's dreams.

The Leiningers, who first thought that all of this was just too incredible, now believe that their son had a past life as James M. Houston Jr. and that he came back because he wasn't finished with something. The Leiningers met with Houston's sister, Anne Barron, and she believes it as well. Little James's recollections are starting to fade as he gets older; however, among his prized possessions are two gifts sent to him by pilot James Houston's sister—a bust of George Washington and a model of a Corsair aircraft that were among the personal effects of James Houston.

Charles Gibson, the host of *ABC News Prime Time*, concluded that one out of every four Americans—Christians and Jews alike—believe that souls do return again in different bodies. The heartwarming story about little James Leininger and former World War II pilot James M. Houston Jr. has been documented in *Soul Survivor*, a book by the Leiningers. The ABC News report may be viewed on the Internet at You Tube—"Reincarnation, Past Life Evidence, parts 1 and 2."

Chapter 11

Angels

The Bible uses the term "angel" to describe a being of divine, godlike character that serves as a messenger of God. A being of divine character may exist in either *spiritual* or *physical* form. The Bible refers to divine beings as "angels" or "gods."

Angels are generally thought of as spiritual beings that exist in heaven. However, angels may also exist in physical form. Angels (beings of divine character) are born on earth to carry out God's will on earth. The Bible's patriarchs, all of whom were able to directly communicate with God, certainly were examples of divine beings serving God on earth. In our modern time, Mother Teresa comes to mind as an angelic being that was sent to earth to manifest God's love for the suffering children of the world.

Angels are often depicted with wings. This symbolizes that they are beings that are not bound by worldly desires. Altruistic love for humankind best characterizes angelic beings, and Jesus is a perfect example of someone of altruistic love who was sent to earth to fulfill God's will.

The idea of "fallen angels" has gained in interest, although the term does not appear anywhere in the Bible. "Fallen" may be associated with Genesis 6:4: "There were giants in the earth in those days; and also after that, when the sons of God came in unto the daughters of men, and they bare children to them, the same became mighty men which were of old, men of renown." Perhaps it was thought that when the sons of God descended to earth to commingle with the daughters of men, they "fell"—literally and figuratively—from their high estate to cohabitate on the lower realm of the earth. It appears a plausible interpretation, and it may have been a part of God's plan. By sharing genetics, their offspring—being half sons of God lineage—"became mighty men of renown." Thus, mankind's abilities made a sudden advance toward divinity.

Angels have also been commonly associated with "guardian angels." Guardian angels, or more correctly guardian spirits, are spiritual beings that are assigned to watch over and guide an individual, and they are usually not the same as the angelic messengers of God. Guardian spirits are of a spiritual level slightly above the spiritual level of the person over whom they have been assigned to watch. Being spiritually "higher" allows them to "see" further ahead, making it possible to give guidance and warnings of impending danger, etc. Guardian spirits are usually the spirits of ancestors or close relatives, and they never attach themselves to the living. The Bible refers to spirits that attach themselves to the living as "demons."

Chapter 12

Demons

The word "demon" comes from the Greek *daimon*, which means simply "a spirit." The New Testament of the Bible describes demons as "unclean spirits" and "devils" that "possess" or attach to people, causing all types of physical and mental illnesses.

Scripture does not reveal what types of spirits make up demons; however, Matthew 8:28-32 reveals that some demons are able to speak, which suggests that some demons may be the spirits of deceased people:

> And when he was come to the other side into the country of the Gergescenes, there met him two possessed with devils, coming out of the tombs, exceeding fierce, so that no man might pass by that way. And, behold, they cried out, saying, What have we to do with thee, Jesus, thou son of God? Art thou come hither to torment us before the time? So the devils besought him, saying, If thou cast us out, suffer us to go away into the herd of swine. And he said unto them, Go. And when they were come out, they went into the herd of swine.

In Matthew 8:28; 9:2-8, 32; 15:30-31; and Mark 3:15; 5:2-20; and 9:17, 25, demons are shown to cause insanity, blindness, deafness, dumbness, palsy, crippled conditions, etc. When Jesus cast out demons, the physical and mental disorders that were being caused by them were also removed, resulting in miraculous healings. This establishes a causal link between spirit attachment or demon possession and the multitude of physical and mental disorders common to the human condition. This can be seen in Matthew 9:32: "As they went out, behold, they brought to him a dumb man possessed with a devil. And when the devil was cast out, the dumb spake."

Why should spirits afflict the living? There are many situations in which people perish with unresolved feelings of revenge and hatred toward those who have caused them to suffer or to lose their lives. Matthew 9:2, 6 reveals that spirit attachment is the direct result of one's sins: "And behold, they brought to him a man sick of the palsy, lying on a bed: and Jesus seeing their faith said unto the sick of the palsy; Son, be of good cheer; thy sins be forgiven thee. But that ye may know that the Son of man hath power on earth to forgive sins. (Then saith he to the sick of the palsy) Arise, take up thy bed, and go unto thine house. And he arose, and departed to his house." When Jesus forgave sins (removed the attaching spirit), the suffering caused by the attaching spirit was also removed. This signified "forgiveness," making atonement for one's sins through suffering no longer necessary because one has been "forgiven" by God.

It may be reasoned that God allows demons to cause suffering as a reflection of God's law, "as ye sow, so shall ye reap," or "do unto others as ye would have others do unto you." That is, demon possession or attachment is one of the ways in which atonement is made for sins (suffering that one has caused others) by experiencing suffering for one's self. It is also the functioning of "free will" granted by God: One may choose to take another's life. Those who lose their life may choose to seek revenge by spiritually attaching themselves to their killers or their killer's descendants. Both choices are obviously against the laws of God and accumulate more sins for those involved. This often results in a continuing cycle of suffering until someone is finally able to "forgive." Thus, to free people from this endless cycle of suffering,

Jesus said, "Love your enemies, bless them that curse you, do good to them that hate you, and pray for them who despitefully use you, and persecute you" (Matthew 5:44).

If demons caused human suffering two thousand years ago, would it be the same today? Modern science has made startling discoveries in this area. In a July 1985 Seven-Day Super Seminar, which took place in Scottsdale, Arizona, some of the world's leading experts on entity attachment met to discuss their research. Presentations from two authorities on entity attachment—Dr. Edith Fiore and William Baldwin—revealed that lapses in memory, fatigue, depression, mood swings, fits of rage, addictions, lust, uncharacteristic behavior, negativity, etc., were telltale symptoms of entity attachment. Their research indicated that seventy to eighty percent of the population suffers from spiritual disturbance. This suggests that only thirty per cent of diseases and afflictions have an actual *physical cause* that may successfully be solved by modern medical science. Perhaps this may explain why certain afflictions do not respond well to medical procedures or are considered incurable because of their spiritual origin.

The Bible reveals that attaching demons or spirits caused various sicknesses and diseases. It would be safe to say that attaching spirits are also causing eighty percent of today's sicknesses and diseases. The book *Mahikari: Thank God for the Answers at Last*, by Dr. A. K. Tebecis, provides a detailed explanation about the phenomenon of disturbance by spirits with a way to resolve it.

Chapter 13

Ghosts

The book of Genesis reveals that God first created heaven (the spiritual realm) and then earth (the physical realm). Thus, spiritual beings were first created in heaven, and then God commanded the earth (nature) to bring forth the appropriate physical form for each spirit to manifest on earth (i.e., God created the spiritual pattern for all earthly beings, and Mother Nature brought forth the appropriate physical body in which the spirit may dwell while on earth).

The manner in which a spirit departs heaven to miraculously appear on earth is called "birth." Thus, the spirit (life force) is the source of animation for all life on earth. At an appropriate time, and equally as miraculous, the spirit will depart the earth to return to its place of origin in heaven. This process of removal is called "death." In this, science and religion may find common ground: science's law of thermodynamics states that energy cannot be created or destroyed; it can only change form. Religion states that life is eternal (i.e., life continues after death).

An observable, universal characteristic of all life on earth is the freedom of movement and action. Scripture refers to this characteristic as the "freedom to choose" that has been granted by God. Thus, the profound eternal message of scripture is that humankind should become ones who can make choices that are in harmony with God's will. To elevate one's self to such a level is said "to become Christlike." To be Christlike is to have overcome human imperfections such as self-centeredness, vanity, conceit, hatred, and anger, etc. Thus, life on earth serves as a "school" for humans to attain Christlike spirits.

It can be seen that humankind demonstrates a wide range of levels in spiritual development. Younger souls are at a primary level, where the focus on "self" dominates. Others may be at a level where "consideration for others" is being practiced. And still others may be at a level where "service to others" is their focus. Whatever level a soul may be working on may be considered as "good" because it is a process of growth that is allowed under the watchful eye of heaven and God.

However, the "freedom to choose" or the freedom to make correct choices provides a constant challenge. Life in the physical world (earth) constantly plays on the desires of the physical body. It is too easy to unconsciously become focused on the material aspects of life and thus become "trapped" in the pursuit of worldly concerns. Many become enthralled with the physical aspects of life, believing that is all there is to existence. When such lives come to an end, the physical world is all that they have known; therefore, their spirits remain earthbound as "ghosts." To guard against this danger, Jesus cautioned, "But lay up for yourselves treasures in heaven. For where your treasure is, there will your heart be also" (Matthew 6:20-21).

A human being consists of spirit, mind, and body interlocked as one entity. At death, the spirit and mind (soul) separate from the physical body to return to their place of origin in the spiritual realm. When a soul remains on earth due to worldly attachments, the living may sometimes see it as a spiritual replica of that person. This spiritual image is what has been called a "ghost." Thus, "ghost" is basically a term for a soul that can be seen by the living—specifically, a term for the earthbound soul of someone that has died but has not returned to its place of origin. Therefore, the term "ghost" carries the negative connotation of something that is not the norm.

Can spirits, such as ghosts, influence the living? Similarly, can guardian angels influence the living? Many state unequivocally that they have been helped by their guardian angels. And there are also those who state unequivocally of being affected by ghosts. Both conditions reveal the existence of the spiritual realm and how closely connected we are to it. Therefore, it is best to be mindful and respectful of everything seen and unseen because separation of the physical and spiritual realms is not always assured.

The phenomenon of ghosts has been recorded in mankind's myths and legends since time immemorial, and it remains a mystery that is not without enormous complexities. Therefore, religions have generally discouraged their followers from delving into this area. Generally speaking, ghosts, or earthbound spirits, are the souls of those who have yet to attain enlightenment—that is, they are souls that are fixated with worldly concerns and desires that prevent them from moving on to their proper place. Perhaps the best that may be said about ghosts is that everything in heaven and earth is God's will, and it is best to understand and to leave things in God's hands.

Chapter 14

Satan

In the beginning (Genesis), God created the powers of fire (manifesting as light, spiritual, vertical, positive, good, etc.) and water (manifesting as darkness, physical, horizontal, negative, evil, etc.).

The universe exists due to the combining (+) of these two basic powers—it being a foundation for God's creative process. When fire and water are in perfect balance (+), harmony, prosperity, and good fortune abound. However, when water (darkness, physical, horizontal, negative, evil) is given priority, then conflict, poverty, and misfortune rule the day.

The term "Satan" represents a personification of the power of water, with its domain being that of the physical realm. This may be interpreted as being separate from God. To enhance this ideology, Satan has been described as a "fallen angel," who rules a domain of suffering called hell. Therefore, when evil is present, it is said that "Satan," or the "devil," is in control.

However, this may be only part of an understanding concerning the universal duality of nature. Scripture reveals that heaven (spiritual) is above and earth (physical) is below. It is said that one goes "up" to heaven and "down" into hell. An inference may be made that hell exists "below" in the physical realm (earth).

When one sees the striking difference between the scriptural description of heaven and the harsh realities of earth, the idea of the existence of hell on earth and Satan being the purveyor of worldly desires may not seem far-fetched. For example, in Matthew 4:8, Jesus was tempted by Satan with kingship over all the kingdoms of the world.

Does Satan exist? The primary power of water constantly functions to maintain balance in the universe and all of its dimensions. The needs and desires of the physical world (earth) weigh constant on mankind. Human imperfections and shortcomings easily give sway to the needs of the material world, causing many to lead lives according to the law of "might makes right," "money talks," and "the end justifies the means" (the law of the jungle). These negative tendencies are realities that testify of the existence of a Satan.

However, mankind has been endowed with the power to choose. Righteous thoughts and desires will call upon the powers of righteousness (God) for assistance. Unrighteous thoughts and desires will call upon the powers of unrighteousness (Satan) for assistance. The Bible's message—and one of the purposes for being—is to become one who can utilize the God-given powers of fire and water in a balanced way (+) and thus fulfill one's purpose on earth in peace and harmony.

In modern terms, this may be translated to "be a self-sufficient contributing member of society" (power of water), *while* "Do unto others as you would have others do unto you" (power of fire). Therefore, when choices must be made—such as choosing between "wealth at the expense of others" or "do unto others as you would have others do unto you"—scripture suggests that priority should be given to "do unto others" conduct. Living in such a way (+) (i.e., combining the "way of the world" with the "way of God"), leaves little room for acknowledging or being influenced by a Satan.

Chapter 15

Heaven and Hell

One of the great mysteries of the Bible concerns the realms of heaven and hell. Scripture defines heaven as a place of eternal joy and happiness and hell as a place of eternal suffering and damnation. Both realms are considered places for the afterlife. However, heaven and hell are also experienced during life on earth, and they appear related to the knowledge of good and evil.

War—characterized by extreme conflict, suffering, and brutality—provides ample evidence that hell exists on earth. Heaven—a state of joy and happiness—also exists on earth. Everyone experiences varying degrees of heaven and hell in daily life. Most hope to avoid the suffering of hell while aspiring to achieve the happiness of heaven. However, challenges in life and the choices that one make often make happiness difficult to attain.

What is happiness (heaven on earth)? Happiness consists of three freedoms:

- freedom from poverty
- freedom from disease
- freedom from strife

"Freedom from poverty" may be understood as having the means to meet one's financial obligations with a little left over. "Freedom from disease" may be understood as having the vitality to accomplish the goals in life. "Freedom from strife" may be understood as living in peace and harmony.

How is "happiness" achieved, and what is its source? The following depiction provides a sense of where one is at and the path toward happiness.

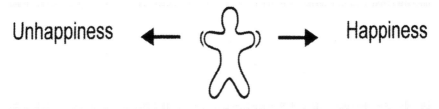

Unhappiness ← ⟵ → Happiness

Thoughts and deeds determine one's direction

At the risk of oversimplification, "happiness" emanates from heaven, and "unhappiness" emanates from hell. Negative thoughts and deeds (sins) cause separation from the happiness of heaven and draw one closer to the unhappiness of hell. Thus, in Matthew 5:28, Jesus said, "But I say unto you, That whosoever looketh on a woman to lust after her hath committed adultery with her already in his heart." This reveals that impure thoughts are recorded as deeds that will manifest as unhappiness and misfortune. This curious arrangement by God reveals how powerful the mind and one's thoughts can be. Thoughts (freedom to choose good or evil) determine one's state of happiness or unhappiness. Thus, common negative endeavors such as judging, complaining, and backbiting all lead to the realm of unhappiness (hell).

However, unhappiness and misfortune are not ends in themselves. They serve as a sign that one's life is heading in the wrong direction and that a change should be made. Unhappiness and misfortune are also a means of compensation to cleanse the sins from one's soul. A purer soul will naturally be drawn closer to the happiness of heaven. This arrangement is a reflection of God's strictness and love. Jesus said in a parable:

> But I say unto you, That ye resist not evil [Evil that is done against you]: but whosoever shall smite thee on thy right cheek, turn to him the other also. And if any man will sue thee at the law, and take away thy coat, let him have thy cloak also. Give to him that asketh thee, and from him that would borrow of thee turn not thou away. Love your enemies, bless them that curse you, do good to them that hate you, and pray for them which despitefully use you, and persecute you; that ye may be the children of your Father which is in heaven. For if ye forgive men their trespasses, your heavenly Father will also forgive you (Matthew 5).

The arrangement to cleanse impurities represents a universal principle that was established at the time of the creation of heaven and earth to provide for the eternal flourishing of God's creation. Therefore, it transcends race, gender, nationality, and religious beliefs. From a spiritual perspective, suffering and misfortune are blessings in disguise that result in better tomorrows and being closer to God.

To help mankind harmonize with this principle, guidelines were given to help avoid needless transgressions. These guidelines were codified in writings such as the Ten Commandments, the Golden Rule, the Beatitudes (Latin *beatus* meaning happy, fortunate, blissful), etc. Thus, "happiness" and "unhappiness" are the result of one's own making, and the thought that happiness can be acquired through material things or from others may be found totally lacking.

Ignorance is never bliss when it concerns the laws of God. This is exemplified by today's younger generation. Being the most materially blessed has caused them to be virtually blind concerning spiritual matters. Concepts such as "honor thy father and mother," virtue, morality, decorum, etc., have all but been forgotten. However, the laws of God persist, and violating such laws will cause transgressors to descend toward misfortune and unhappiness. Therefore, it is vital to know and follow the rules of life (the laws of God/how the universe works) to be successful in life. Being aware of the principle of happiness and unhappiness is an important first step to achieve success.

Chapter 16

Sex and the Bible

Through science, sex may be understood as a biological function for the reproduction of species. Through religion, sex may be understood as the means by which life may appear in the physical world (earth). Sexual desire may be seen as God-given to ensure the perpetuation of species. Through these basic understandings, God's intent concerning sex and the perpetuation of life on earth may be realized.

Whereas the laws of nature in virtually all life-forms control the act of reproduction, human sexuality is unique in that humans possess the knowledge of good and evil (free will/not controlled by nature), and humans are considered children of God. Therefore, the Bible contains important passages concerning God's guidance for proper sexual conduct as well as examples of conduct that violate God's will. In Leviticus 18:1-3 is written, "And the Lord spake unto Moses, saying, Speak unto the children of Israel, and say unto them, I am the Lord your God. After the doings of the land of Egypt, wherein ye dwelt, shall ye not do: and after the doings of the land of Canaan, whither I bring you, shall ye not do: neither shall ye walk in their ordinances." That is, conduct/ practices considered normal in one culture may not be found acceptable in the eyes of God—for example, the peculiar sexual practices of the cities of Sodom and Gomorrah in the book of Genesis, chapter 19, that were considered abhorrent.

This appears related to today's modern age of technology in which materialism (the pursuit of money, convenience, and physical pleasure) dominates, and spiritual wisdom is subordinate. Thus, human sexuality is now viewed in strong physical terms, often as a source of pleasure without limits or restrictions. When relationships are established in an unbalanced way, the meaning of love and fidelity is obscured, and this results in unstable unions that culminate in misfortune and unhappiness.

To help obviate suffering, the book of Leviticus gives specific guidance to the children of God concerning the proper function of human sexuality, which scripture terms "uncovering thy nakedness." Leviticus 18:6-18 records God's guidance concerning proper sexual conduct with "near of kin."

Leviticus 18:6: "None of you shall approach to any that is near of kin to him, to uncover their nakedness."

Leviticus 18:7: "The nakedness of thy father, or the nakedness of thy mother, shalt thou not uncover: she is thy mother."

Leviticus 18:8: "The nakedness of thy father's wife shalt thou not uncover: it is thy father's nakedness."

Leviticus 18:9: "The nakedness of thy sister, the daughter of thy father, or daughter of thy mother, whether she be born at home, or born abroad, even their nakedness thou shalt not uncover."

Leviticus 18:10: "The nakedness of thy son's daughter, or of thy daughter's daughter, even their nakedness thou shalt not uncover: for theirs is thine own nakedness."

Leviticus 18:11: "The nakedness of thy father's wife's daughter, begotten of thy father, she is thy sister, thou shalt not uncover her nakedness."

Leviticus 18:12: "Thou shalt not uncover the nakedness of thy father's sister: she is thy father's near kinswoman."

Leviticus 18:13: "Thou shalt not uncover the nakedness of thy mother's sister: for she is thy mother's near kinswoman."

Leviticus 18:14: "Thou shalt not uncover the nakedness of thy father's brother, thou shalt not approach to his wife: she is thine aunt."

Leviticus 18:15: "Thou shalt not uncover the nakedness of thy daughter-in-law: she is thy son's wife; thou shalt not uncover her nakedness."

Leviticus 18:16: "Thou shalt not uncover the nakedness of thy brother's wife: it is thy brother's nakedness."

Leviticus 18:17: "Thou shalt not uncover the nakedness of a woman and her daughter, neither shalt thou take her son's daughter, or her daughter's daughter, to uncover her nakedness; for they are her near kinswoman: it is wickedness."

Leviticus 18:18: "Neither shalt thou take a wife to her sister, to vex here, to uncover her nakedness, beside the other in her lifetime."

Leviticus 18:19-23 records God's guidance concerning peculiar sexual conduct.

Leviticus 18:19: "Also thou shalt not approach unto a woman to uncover her nakedness, as long as she is put apart for her uncleanness." (This may be a reference to a woman's menses or contagion.)

Leviticus 18:20: "Moreover thou shalt not lie carnally with thy neighbor's wife, to defile thyself with her."

Leviticus 18:21: "And thou shalt not let any of thy seed pass through the fire to Molech, neither shalt thou profane the name of thy God: I am the Lord." (Could this be a reference to sexual acts that are beyond the function of reproduction?)

Leviticus 18:22: "Thou shalt not lie with mankind, as with womankind: it is abomination." (This controversial verse clearly condemns *sexual acts* between men and between women—it does not condemn personal relationships or the nature that one has been born with.)

Leviticus 18:23: "Neither shalt thou lie with any beast to defile thyself therewith: neither shall any woman stand before a beast to lie down thereto: it is confusion."

Leviticus 18:24-30 records God's guidance concerning the violation of righteous sexual conduct.

Leviticus 18:24: "Defile not ye yourselves in any of these things: for in all these the nations are defiled which I cast out before you."

Leviticus 18:25: "And the land is defiled: therefore I do visit the iniquity thereof upon it, and the land itself vomiteth out her inhabitants." (It is of interest that science has proposed a Gaia hypothesis that holds the earth to be a single, self-regulating complex system; and Native Americans refer to the earth as the Earth Mother, who lives, breathes, and feels. Could natural disasters be a manner in which "the land itself vomiteth out her inhabitants"?)

Leviticus 18:26: "Ye shall therefore keep my statutes and my judgments, and shall not commit any of these abominations; neither any of your own nation, nor any stranger that sojourneth among you." (It is significant to note that "shalt not commit any of these abominations" refers to certain heterosexual and homosexual acts equally as abominations.)

Leviticus 18:27: "For all these abominations have the men of the land done, which were before you, and the land is defiled."

Leviticus 18:28: "That the land spew not you out also, when ye defile it, as it spewed out the nations that were before you."

Leviticus 18:29: "For whosoever shall commit any of these abominations, even the souls that commit them shall be cut off from among their people." (This may refer to subconscious guilt that may cause transgressors to unknowingly become withdrawn and aloof—thus, being "cut off from among their people.")

Leviticus 18:30: "Therefore shall ye keep mine ordinance, that ye commit not any one of these abominable customs, which were committed before you, and that ye defile not yourselves therein: I am the Lord your God."

These verses from the book of Leviticus may resonate with many as things to be revisited and incorporated into one's life to achieve spiritual elevation and oneness with God. To those strongly influenced by the ways of the materialistic world, these verses may appear antiquated and incredulous. However, the manner in which scripture may be received is a reflection of the freedom to choose that has been granted by God.

A point of confusion concerns the modern use and meaning of the word "love," in which there are many "forms" of love— such as romantic love, platonic love, physical love, etc. From this perspective, all forms of love are perfunctorily considered the same. However, scripture presents a different perspective. It suggests, written between its lines, that the true meaning of love is the *altruistic love* demonstrated by one's heavenly Parent. This leads to the conclusion that other "forms" of love are more the murmuring of the material world—tending to confuse and render the words of God unheeded—rather than the Truth.

An esoteric principle known among some of the world's spiritual masters is that an increase in sexual desire is a telltale sign of one being disturbed by spirits. The exercise of sexual desire decreases one's life force, thus allowing negative spirits (the Bible's demons, devil, Satan, unclean spirits) to gain greater control over an individual.

In today's materialistic age—in which the physical aspect of love is emphasized to the extreme and impropriety is becoming the norm—it is fortuitous to be aware and avoid such pitfalls.

Chapter 17

Forgiveness

"For if ye forgive men their trespasses, your heavenly Father will also forgive you: But if ye forgive not men their trespasses, neither will your Father forgive your trespasses" (Matthew 6:14-15).

This quotation provides a deeply profound revelation concerning the essence of forgiveness: "For if ye forgive men their trespasses, your heavenly Father will also forgive you" indicates that forgiveness *must first come from another* (the one who has been trespassed) before forgiveness can come from God. That is, "We are not forgiven until we have been forgiven by those whom we have caused to suffer." This reveals the necessity for atonement in some way.

This truism, however plain or simple, often challenges the logic of mere mortals due to the limited capacity of human wisdom to "see" beyond one's present circumstance or to exercise unbiased thought. "How can I forgive someone for hurting me for no reason?" Or, "How can I forgive them after all they have done to me?" Such conundrums surely are nothing more than the reaping of what has been sown or the returning of one's own doing.

Therefore, it may be helpful to view forgiveness not as a mental or verbal endeavor, but rather as a feeling akin to the removal of negativity from one's heart. A saying is that "time heals old wounds"; thus, forgiveness is often achieved over a period of time—that is, according to God's timetable. The following is an example of how forgiveness may work. Due to some mysterious reason (God works in mysterious ways), one may have vague, unexplainable negative feelings toward another person, and these negative feelings cause one to badly mistreat that person. Fortunately, the person that has been mistreated does not respond in kind, nor displays any ill will—perhaps they may even accept mistreatment with goodwill. Under such conditions, one's negative feelings for that person will gradually dissipate (God works in mysterious ways) and may even turn into respect for that person. *The removal of negative feelings from one's heart is called "forgiveness."*

The negative feelings that were in one's heart may be best described as a spiritual matter (grudge) that was held against the soul of the mistreated person. Thus, after satisfying one's grudge (removing the negativity in one's heart), there is no longer any desire to mistreat that person further, and—letting bygones be bygones—both may go their separate ways in peace. And this is of great significance because by releasing negativity, one is brought a step closer to God, and this incredible blessing was all made possible by the behavior of the person that was being mistreated: They humbly, with unquestioning childlike obedience, accepted mistreatment by following God's guidance: "But I say unto you, Love your enemies, bless them that curse you, do good to them that hate you, and pray for them which despitefully use you, and persecute you: That ye may be the children of your Father which is in heaven" (Matthew 5:44-45).

And the mistreated person, having atoned for a spiritual debt by humbly enduring mistreatment (reaping what they had sown), will have negativity removed from his or her heart as well, which will also move him or her a step closer to God. Through the mysterious principle of forgiveness, humankind may work together, serving as persecutor and persecuted, and vice versa, to rise spiritually, step by step, closer to God and entrance into heaven.

Viewing "forgiveness" from this overall perspective may provide the realization that confrontations are usually spiritual in origin. That is, both parties are working on issues from their forgotten past. Therefore, when one can give forgiveness—not with the feeling of being justified, but rather with the heart of sincere apology and gratitude—then God shall forgive one.

Judging with human wisdom is to follow the "way of the world," with grudge and resentment. Following Matthew 5:44-45 is to follow the "way of God."

Chapter 18
Thou Shalt Not Judge

"Judge not, that ye be not judged. For with what judgment ye judge, ye shall be judged: and with what measure ye mete, it shall be measured to you again" (Matthew 7:1-2).

The admonishment to **not judge others**, although not one of the Ten Commandments, is of equal importance due to its grievous nature: judging others can be seen as an affront and encroachment of God's authority. It is an egregious transgression that has become almost second nature to man.

A telltale sign of "judging" is the emergence of negativity and anger in one's heart that stems from the self-centeredness of one's own narrow point of view (e.g., faultfinding). To judge others is the antithesis of altruistic love. Negativity within one's heart (a reflection of sin) is what separates one from God and heaven.

In contrast, "discernment"—the ability see things from another point of view—engenders understanding and compassion (e.g., being understanding and forgiving of another's predicament). A greater step forward would be to see things from God's point of view: "what is God trying to show me—possibly about myself?" Or, "could this be an opportunity for atonement to cleans and elevate my soul? Developing the ability to discern is what should be strived for to maintain a pure heart and achieve elevation of one's soul.

The practice of judging others may be considered a "way of the world." As such, it is often committed unknowingly without much thought. However, one should awaken and strive to overcome the tendency to judge (i.e., to assume God's authority) by nurturing discernment (i.e., the ability to fulfill God's will with gratitude and compassion).

To help achieve this, scripture admonishes: "And why beholdest thou the mote that is in thy brother's eye, but considerest not the beam that is in thine own eye? Thou hypocrite, first cast out the beam that is in thine own eye; and then shalt thou see clearly to cast out the mote out of thy brother's eye" (Matthew 7:3-5).

Chapter 19

The Creation of
Adam and Eve

The creation of man begins in Genesis 2:4-6: "These are the generations of the heavens and of the earth when they were created, in the day that the Lord God formed man of the dust of the ground, and breathed into his nostrils the breath of life; and man became a living soul." Whereas God commanded the earth to "bring forth," or materialize, all of the flora and fauna that he had created, it was God himself who brought forth (materialized) man. "Of the dust of the ground" refers to man's physical body. "Dust" may be a reference to an existing material (life-form, primate) previously brought forth by the earth. "Formed" may be a reference to genetic manipulation and/or divine intervention to make man a unique human entity.

The use of the term *Lord God* appears to refer to a deity other than the Creator. It is likely that Lord God was an elder of the divine hierarchy of heaven who was sent to appear in physical form on earth to directly carry out the formation of man's physical body—that is, to create a physical body appropriate to house the soul of God's child, allowing him to rule the earth in place of God. "And breathed into his nostrils the breath of life; and man became a living soul" indicates that primate man was transformed into a human being, endowed with consciousness and the unlimited potential of his Creator.

The science of genetics has revealed that, although sharing a common origin, primates are distinct and are not shown to have evolved from one another (i.e., man did not naturally evolve from apes). Researcher Lloyd Pye's "Intervention Theory" indicates that, although humans share a remarkable similarity with the chromosomal makeup of other primates, such as chimpanzees, gorillas, and orangutans, humans carry only forty-six chromosomes while all other primates carry forty-eight. The two-chromosome difference in humans was found to be caused by a careful and deliberate fusing of the second and third chromosomes in humans. This type of genetic modification was found to be similar to the procedure used by today's geneticists in their labs.

Did physical beings (servants of God) genetically manipulate an earthly primate (dust of the ground) to create a being with all of the necessary physical properties (large brain, bifocal eyes, legs, arms, and hands with opposable thumbs, etc.) necessary to serve as God's magistrate? And once such a physical being had been created, did God direct souls to enter such a being (and breath into his nostrils the breath of life; and man became a living soul), thereby creating the human being, or child of God? The Bible clearly states that God created man. Science has yet to find a "missing link" demonstrating that humans naturally evolved from ape-like creatures. Instead, science finds the sudden appearance of humans in the anthropologic records that coincide with the Bible's account that humans were created by divine intervention (i.e., humans were physically and spiritually created by God and were not a product of nature, such as other life-forms on earth).

The account of man's creation continues in Genesis 2:8-9: "And the Lord God planted a garden eastward in Eden; and there he put the man whom he had formed. And out of the ground made the Lord God to grow every tree that is pleasant to the sight, and good for food; the tree of life also in the midst of the garden, and the tree of knowledge of good and evil." Genesis 2:25: "And they were both naked, the man and his wife, and were not ashamed."

"Naked and not ashamed" indicates that Adam and Eve were unschooled primates for which God provided everything: every tree that is good for food to nurture his body, the tree of life to nurture his soul, and the tree of knowledge of good and evil to nurture his mind. Man was innocent (primitive) and would need to acquire the necessary skills to rule the world in place of God.

The story of Adam and Eve partaking of the tree of knowledge of good and evil allegorically explains how man was prepared to become God's magistrate. Genesis 3:17, 22: "But of the tree of the knowledge of good and evil, thou shalt not eat of it: for in the day that thou eatest thereof thou shalt surely die. And the Lord God said, Behold, the man is become as one of us, to know good and evil: and now, lest he put forth his hand, and take also of the tree of life, and eat, and live for ever."

"Behold, the man is become as one of us, to know good and evil" indicates that man had become a child of God with "free will" and an unlimited potential for development. Acquiring the knowledge of good represented the potential to develop art, music, language, science, technology, benevolence, devotion to God, etc. "Evil" symbolized the opposite potential, for war and man's inhumanity to man. Therefore, to fulfill the role of God's magistrate, man had to be taught—ergo, God placed Cherubim in the Garden of Eden to teach humankind the way of civilization based on the way of God, synonymous with "the way of the tree of life."

The necessity for humans having to be taught is a profound revelation in scripture. It may be assumed that human behavior is a characteristic that is "inborn" or naturally occurring. To the contrary, many accounts of children being raised in the wild by animals suggest things may not be so clear-cut. A case in point is a very well publicized account of two children that were found being raised by wolves near Midnapore in the Bengal jungle of India.

The story began in the year 1920. A priest named Rev. Joseph Singh, a missionary in charge of an orphanage, began responding to reports by villagers of ghostly figures seen traveling at night with a band of wolves in the area. They were described as human-like creatures that moved about on all fours. Rev. Singh was able to determine the location of the wolves' lair, and with the help of a large hunting party, broke into the lair, where two human children, along with two wolf cubs, were found.

The children turned out to be two girls about three and five years of age. They did not appear to be sisters, and it was theorized that the wolves had adapted them at different times. The girls appeared to have no humanness in their behavior, acting and thinking more like wolves, often howling to be set free. Even their senses were keen and animal-like. They could detect the presence of meat even at great distances.

Rev. Singh felt that it was his responsibility to help the girls regain their innate human characteristics. Repatriating the girls—the elder christened Kamala and the younger Amala—was long and difficult. Initially, they would tear off any clothes put on them and would only eat raw meat. Their bodies had adjusted to the years of running on all fours, making it impossible for them to walk upright. They never smiled or expressed interest in other humans. The human voice seemed strange and uninteresting to them, so progress to teach them was very slow.

Unfortunately, before Rev. Singh had made much progress, the younger girl, Amala, became ill and died. Before her death, Amala was able to mimic human speech with babbling and cooing, the first stage of speech development in a normal child. Amala's death proved to be a great setback for the elder girl, Kamala, who went through a long period of mourning in which it was feared that she would also pass away. However, she eventually recovered and gradually began the work of losing her wolf-like characteristics.

Over a period of time, physical therapy was used to help Kamala loosen her malformed ligaments, and that allowed her to stand and walk in an upright position. However, she was never able to fully walk naturally and would revert to running on all fours. Eventually, Kamala began to adopt other human characteristics, such as eating normal food, sleeping with the children in the orphanage, and being comfortable around other humans. However, speech development was much more difficult. After three years of tutoring, Kamala was able to master a small vocabulary of about a dozen words, increasing that to forty words after several more years. Although her words were not fully formed, and her grammar was stilted, Kamala's progress—considering that she was no more than a wolf cub several years earlier—was taken as a first sign of social development and awareness, albeit far short of the speech and development of normally reared children. Whether Kamala would have regained all of her human skills will never be known. Sadly, Kamala passed away in 1929 as a result of illness. However, her developing humanness was reflected by a warm relationship with Rev. Singh's wife, addressing her as "Mama."

Scripture (Genesis 3) reveals that man was created in God's image with the power to choose good or evil. However, "lest he put forth his hand and take also of the tree of life" (the way of civilization based on God), he shall surely die without eternal life.

The way in which man "puts forth his hand and takes of the tree of life" is by being taught the way of civilization by parents—who were taught by their parents, who were taught by their parents' parents, ad infinitum to Adam and Eve, who were taught by God.

In the story of Amala and Kamala, Rev. Singh and his wife were in the process of teaching the children the way of civilization before the children's unfortunate passing. Thus, the children were unable to fulfill their potential as human beings. That is, they were unable to participate as contributing members of society, or to worship or offer service to God.

It is of interest that, of the Ten Commandments, the commandment to honor thy father and thy mother is preceded, in order of importance, only by the commandments that honor God.

Chapter 20

Cain and Abel

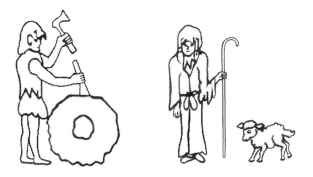

Cain and Abel, the first offspring of Adam and Eve, were patriarchs of the two basic types of humans created on earth. The firstborn, Cain, represented humans endowed with the desire and ability to develop the material wealth of the earth. Genesis 4:2, 17, 20, 21, 22 describe Cain as being "a tiller of the soil" and his descendants as "builder of a city . . . the father of such as dwell in tents and have cattle . . . the father of all such as handle the harp and organ . . . an instructor of every artificer in brass and iron."

The second-born, Abel, represented humans endowed with the desire and ability to nurture spiritual development. Genesis 4:2 describes Abel as "a keeper of sheep."

Without Cain (people with a strong material desire to develop the wealth of the earth), humankind would remain in a primitive condition with little potential for advancement, and there would be little joy in life. Without Abel (people with a strong desire to nurture others), humankind would develop an overly materialistic civilization with the potential to destroy the world because of the lack of love and caring for others.

Thus, Cain and Abel represented the original counterparts or "soul mates" of humankind, and it would appear that it was God's intent that Cain and Abel should work together—each contributing his unique abilities—for the advancement of mankind. Through the effort of Cain, man could utilize the benefits of civilization. Through the effort of Abel, man could live in a God-centered society based on love and harmony.

In Genesis 4:3-5: "Cain brought of the fruit of the ground an offering to the Lord" and "Abel, he also brought of the firstlings of his flock." "And the Lord had respect unto Abel and to his offering: But unto Cain and to his offering he had not respect." This indicates that God places priority on spiritual growth ("firstlings of his flock") rather than on material wealth ("fruit of the ground").

The Bible's revelation concerning this point indicates that mankind should combine both attributes—material development and spiritual growth—in balanced harmony, with priority placed on cultivating spiritual growth. It is when priority is placed on material development (the pursuit of wealth, power, prestige, etc.) that mankind experiences disease, poverty, and misfortune.

Genesis 4:8, 25 states that God gave the world Seth to replace the slain Abel, who died by the hands of his brother. Through the lineage of Seth appear the Bible's patriarchs, prophets, servants, and savior (the Good Shepherd).

The formal record designating the lineage of Cain essentially ends with chapter four of the book of Genesis. However, the descendants of Cain can be seen represented throughout the Bible as kings, world rulers, captains of industry, and as Christ's counterpart.

Both lineages continue to this day, each contributing toward the progress of the world. The Bible focuses on man's spiritual lineage (Abraham, Isaac, Jacob, Messiah, etc.); however, the Bible has been brought forth through the effort of all humankind.

Chapter 21

The Garden of Eden

"Eden" is an ancient word that defines the Earth as being an extension of heaven. Genesis 2:8 states: "And the Lord God planted a garden eastward in Eden." That is to say, God established a garden in the eastern part of the earth.

The earth is divided into eastern and western halves. The eastern half begins at zero degrees longitude at Greenwich, England, and extends eastward to 180 degrees longitude at the international date line in the central Pacific Ocean. Thus, the Garden of Eden was situated in an area somewhere between Greenwich, England, and the middle of the Pacific Ocean.

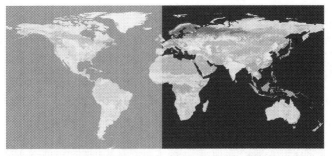

Eastern Hemisphere

Genesis 2:8 continues: "And there he put the man whom he had formed." This indicates that man first appeared in the Garden of Eden, somewhere in the eastern half of the world.

Genesis 3:4 continues: "So he drove out the man; and he placed at the east of the Garden of Eden Cherubims, and a flaming sword which turned every way, to keep the way of the tree of life." This verse states that, after Adam and Eve were cast out of the Garden of Eden, God placed Cherubim at the east end of the garden. The word "Cherubim" is derived from the Hebrew word, *kerubh*, which describes a winged, celestial figure regarded as a guardian of a sacred place and a servant of God. The term "winged" designates a god (divine soul) manifesting as a physical being. Jesus is an example of a great, divine soul (Son of God) who appeared on earth as a physical being (Son of man).

The term "flaming sword," is a metaphor for the words of God (i.e., the heavenly principles or laws that guide humankind toward eternal life). "Which turned every way," describes the spreading of the words of God throughout the world from its origin at the "east of the Garden of Eden." "The flaming sword which turned every way" is synonymous with "the light that shines from the East."

The "flaming sword which turned every way" became an emblem to show humankind where the words of God could be found. The following depiction illustrates the origin of this emblem.

 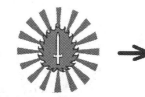 

Flaming Sword   Which Turned Everyway   Ensign For Mankind

Cherubim Seal

"To keep the way of the tree of life" refers to the Cherubim serving as caretakers and disseminators of the words of God. Being divine in origin, they served as exemplars, showing humankind how to live as children of God. The Cherubim taught humankind benevolence and devotion to God as well as the ways of civilization (the arts, music, language, agriculture, science, technology, etc.). This explains how advances in ancient cultures could suddenly appear, as well as why there are many traditions that speak of someone, in the ancient past, coming to teach civilization and devotion to a single God. The birth of all of the great civilizations of the world were based on "the way of the tree of life" disseminated by the Cherubim from the Garden of Eden. The following Egyptian artifacts reveal their influence.

Sekhmet

Cherubim Seal

The Goddess Sekhmet (Metropolitan Museum of Art, New York) is depicted with the head of a lioness to signify fearlessness to defend, nurture, and protect her charge. The solar disk above her head, along with the serpent, designates her as a goddess/ servant of the Most High God. The seals on her breast identify her as being the source of the way of the tree of life and as a Cherub sent from the Garden of Eden to nurture the budding Egyptian empire.

Tutankhamun Dagger   Cherubim Seal

The Cherubim seals on Tutankhamun's scabbard designate him as a Cherub that was sent from the Garden of Eden to guide the Egyptian empire. The two seals, appearing as flowers emanating from the lotus plant (the lotus was symbolic of the Mu continent), reveal the Cherubim springing forth from the Garden of Eden. The youngling above the seals represents mankind being nurtured by the way of the tree of life as disseminated by the Cherubim from the Garden of Eden.

The Cherubim were the first divine representatives of God on earth. The modern term, emperor, is descriptive of the role that the Cherubim fulfilled as divine representatives sent to appear on earth. It can be said that the Cherubim were the world's first emperor and empress, who were sent by God to guide *all humankind* toward fulfilling God's will on earth and achieving eternal life in heaven. The Bible reveals that God placed Cherubim at the east of the Garden of Eden. Where the Cherubim—the world's first lineage of emperors and empresses—can be found would indicate the location of the Garden of Eden.

In *Mahikari: Thank God for the Answers at Last*, its author Dr. A. K. Tebecis, stated that startling new geological evidence presented by Dr. M. Yamaguchi at a conference of the Japanese Geological Society dates the age of Japan as being 3.7 billion years old, the time when the earth's crust is thought to have formed. Dr. Tebecis also writes that a traditional belief among the Japanese people is that the emperor of Japan (Cherubim?) is a descendant of God, and that ultra, ancient records (Flaming Sword?) are maintained at the Imperial Ancestor's Main Shrine in Ise (biblical "Jesse"?), Japan.

In Germany's Cologne Cathedral can be found one of the oldest Western depictions of the crucified Christ. Named the Gero Cross (after Gero, the archbishop of Cologne who commissioned it in 965-970 AD), the figure of Christ measures 187 cm high and 165 cm wide. Of particular interest is the emblem behind the head of Christ. It is a rendering of the sixteen-petal chrysanthemum seal with a cross in its center. This emblem signifies the unique relationship between Christ, the Cherubim of the Garden of Eden and the True Living God. It is of interest that Jesus's lineage is traced back to King David of Israel and to "Jesse."

Gero Cross   Christ and Cherubim Seal

Genesis 2:10 continues: "And a river went out of Eden to water the garden, and from thence it was parted, and became into four heads." This reveals that mankind originated in the Garden of Eden. "And from thence it was parted, and became into four heads" reveals that four world ages of man would originate from the Garden of Eden—each world age ending by cataclysms of nature (e.g., one destruction being recorded in the Bible as the Great Flood of Noah).

The ancient records of man, maintained throughout the world by various aboriginal cultures, such as the Maya and Hopi of the Americas, also record these end-of-an-age events. The ancient records of the Hopi say that the Garden of Eden sank beneath the sea during the end of the fourth world age. It is worth noting that two of the world's great civilizations, the kingdoms of Israel and Judah, also mysteriously disappeared at a similar time in the Bible—ergo, secular history's fabled empires of Mu (Israel) and Atlantis (Judah).

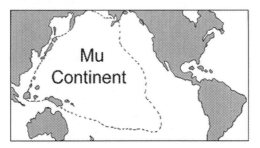

The Fabled Lost Continent of Mu: The Garden of Eden?

The ancient records (clay tablets in India) that were translated by the late Colonel James Churchward (February 27, 1851, to January 4, 1936) speak of a paradisiacal land on which man was created and from which mankind's great civilizations flourished. This mysterious land called Mu was situated in the Pacific Ocean, and it was destroyed by cataclysms of nature—being submerged beneath the sea—nearly twelve thousand years ago.

A recent discovery of undersea megalithic structures off the coast of Okinawa revealed pyramid-like structures, temples, statues, avenues, and ancient hieroglyphs. These artifacts lend credence to the existence of a great civilization that once existed in the Pacific Ocean. The records from India state that the remnants of Mu, after its destruction, were the islands in the Pacific Ocean and the islands of Japan.

The Garden of Eden and the lost continent of Mu are of great significance due to a geographical and historical relationship with the ancient kingdom of Israel. Colonel Churchward's research has been preserved in a series of books on the lost continent of Mu. The ancient records—such as the records of the Hopi and the records from India—help establish a chronological and geographical connection with the events that transpired in the Old Testament of the Bible.

The Garden of Eden was the cradle of civilization from which mankind first appeared and then populated the earth. Thus, when mankind was cast out from the Garden of Eden, civilization would have spread eastward toward Asia and westward toward the Americas, eventually encircling the earth and possibly culminating with the northern and southern Egyptian empires—these civilizations being the last of the pyramid builders. This pattern of migration appears to be supported by recent archaeological findings by University of South Carolina archaeologist Dr. Albert Goodyear, as reported in *Science Daily* (November 18, 2004). Ancient stone tools unearthed along the Savannah River in Allendale County, South Carolina, were found in carbonized plant remains that were radiocarbon dated to be at least fifty thousand years old. This places modern man in North America long before the establishment of the Egyptian civilization, which is estimated to have originated about fifteen thousand years ago.

A hallmark of ultra-ancient civilizations was their megalithic stone structures, especially the pyramid. Many pyramids have recently been discovered in China, Japan, and the Americas. The stone structures found submerged in the Pacific Ocean off the coast of Japan have created the greatest interest among scientists. The most studied and photographed structure has been the six-hundred-feet-wide and ninety-feet-high Yonaguni underwater megalith, located off the coast of Yonaguni-jima, near Okinawa.

Discovered in 1986 by dive tour director Kihachiro Aratake, the site has revealed structures that appear to be the ruins of a once thriving ancient civilization. Dr. Masaaki Kimura, professor of marine geology at the University of the Ryukus, was one of the first to lead a scientific expedition to explore the Yonaguni site. Their discoveries included artifacts of what appear to be pyramids, cities, roads, monuments, and hieroglyphs. Could the Yonaguni structures be the remnants of the fabled lost continent of Mu?

Do the presence of ultra-ancient structures (e.g., Monk's Mound pyramid in Cahokia, Illinois; pyramid in Teotihuacan, Mexico; the pyramids of Shaanxi Province, China; and the many pyramids throughout Japan) lend credence to the biblical account of where civilization originated and to where it spread throughout the world?

Archaeological evidence and Genesis 3:24 strongly suggest that the site of the Bible's Garden of Eden would be situated in the area of Japan. Also, a recent History Channel television documentary on the Garden of Eden reported that in 1266 AD, European explorer Marco Polo, in a quest to find the fabled Garden of Eden, traveled to China and was told by Emperor Shizu of the Yuan Dynasty that the Garden of Eden lay at the border of his empire. This would also suggest the area of Japan.

Therefore, the Bible's lands of the patriarchs Abraham, Isaac, and Jacob—the lands to which they would have migrated, when departing the Garden of Eden in the Pacific—would have been eastward, toward North and South America and beyond, and westward toward Asia, India, and beyond. Thus, the lands of their inheritance, as suggested in scripture, would have been the lands of North America (Canaan) and South America (the Land of Milk and Honey). The ancient record of the Americas—an adjunct to the Old Testament—has been preserved in the *Book of Mormon*.

It is of interest that as world history is retraced from Europe back to antiquity, its path leads westward to the ancient civilizations of North and South America and eastward to Asia— and ultimately, to the Garden of Eden, which once existed in the Pacific Ocean.

Chapter 22

The Sons of God
and the Daughters of Man

"And it came to pass, when men began to multiply on the face of the earth, and daughters were born unto them, That the sons of God saw the daughters of men that they were fair; and they took them wives of all which they chose . . . and they bare children to them, the same became mighty men which were of old, men of renown" (Genesis 6:1-2, 4).

These verses reveal the existence of superior beings (the sons of God) that were intimately involved with humankind since the beginning of earth's history. The sons of God were *physical beings* capable of intermarrying and siring children with humans; however, they were superior to the human race—they were not of the earth. Although the Bible does not go into much detail, they obviously were of a high spiritual and technological level and were entrusted with the development of life on earth.

Genesis 1:26 records them saying, "Let us make man in our image, after our likeness." This reveals that man's *physical body* was patterned after the sons of God. In genetic terms, human beings may be considered as kin. However, although appearing physically similar to humans, they were higher in spiritual level than yet-to-attain-divinity humans. Because of this spiritual difference, their offspring—being half sons of God and half daughters of men lineage—became "mighty men which were of old, men of renown."

The Bible reveals that God created the spiritual and physical worlds. The spiritual world is populated by various levels of spiritual beings: The most high is God the Father, followed by elders, lords, archangels, angels, divine souls, and human souls. Earth is the place of training for humans; therefore, the sons of God appeared in physical form to develop a physical body for the expression of the human soul and to teach "the way of the tree of life" (God-centered way of civilization). They were also the source of humankind's knowledge of written language, agriculture, math, science, etc.

Traditions relate humankind's relationship with the sons of God. For example, the Japanese and Native Americans hold the belief that their ancestors came from the stars. Could they be descendants of the sons of God and daughters of man?

The Dogon, natives of West Africa, say that their ancestors were visited by human-like beings from the Sirius constellation that came in a flying craft with tripod landing gear. The visitors taught the Dogon ancestors the way of agriculture, science, and the proper way to live. Of interest was the Dogan knowledge of cosmology. They knew about the surface of the Moon being dry and barren, that there were rings around the planet Saturn, that the Milky Way was a spiral galaxy of stars, and that the planets revolved around the sun. Of particular interest was their knowledge that Sirius consisted of not one, but three stars. Modern science discovered Sirius's second star (Sirius B) in 1862. Could the visitors to the Dogon be the sons of God teaching the ways of God?

Modern science and researchers have also added to the wealth of data that link mankind's ancient past with the stars. In 1964, astronomer Virginia Trimble discovered that a shaft from the king's chamber in the Great Pyramid at Giza pointed to the Orion constellation. It was believed that this would aid the king's return to his place of origin in the constellation of Orion. Also, in a 1994 book, *The Orion Mystery,* authors Robert Bauval and Adrian Gilbert made a further connection between the pyramids at Giza with the Orion constellation. It was discovered that the placement of the three pyramids at Giza, when viewed from above—the larger two pyramids being in alignment and the smaller pyramid being slightly off center—fit the pattern of the three stars in the belt of Orion. It would appear that the forefathers of mankind deliberately left clues that would reveal mankind's true history and connection with the heavens.

Science and the ancient records of mankind's past civilizations are beginning to point toward a universe filled with life that God created. The most precious gift given to humankind was the knowledge of man's relationship with his Creator and the method of worship. The book of Genesis reveals that the children of God constructed megalithic structures (pyramids/holy altars) as monuments to God. Although the Bible does not reveal who taught mankind about such structures or how they were built, it would be safe to say that it was the sons of God who taught/aided mankind with the building of such awesome structures.

Modern science has begun to explore the earth's solar system. In 1976, a NASA Viking Orbiter-1 craft photographed portions of the surface of the planet Mars. Several photographic images revealed the existence of a face—measuring 1.6 miles long, 1.2 miles wide and 2,000 feet high—that resembled an Egyptian pharaoh. The photos also revealed pyramids. These structures appear to be similar to ones constructed on Earth in the distant past. This suggests that the sons of God were given the mission to spread life throughout the universe. Also, images on Earth that are only visible from the air (e.g., the huge drawings of animals, insects, humanoids, etc.) on the Nazca Plain, Peru, and the huge head of a Native American in Canada (Google Earth 50 0'38. 20"N 110 6'48. 32"W) also suggest that the Bible's sons of God were visitors from the stars.

Jesus expressed a similar theme that the sons of God were not of this earth. When being confronted by his persecutors, he said, "Ye are from beneath; I am from above: ye are of this world; I am not of this world" (John 8:23).

It is curious that there are some who consider the sons of God as ominous "aliens" from outer space, while others consider them to be their ancestors and mentors from distant stars, who promised one day to return.

Chapter 23

Noah's Flood

An important function of scripture is to impart the spiritual significance of biblical events. This is clearly demonstrated in the great flood of Noah.

The book of Genesis, chapters 6-9, chronicles the destruction of all life on earth as a result of the proliferation of evil and corruption on earth. Genesis 6:5, 7, 12:

> And God saw that the wickedness of man was great in the earth, and that every imagination of the thoughts of his heart was only evil continually.
>
> And the Lord said, I will destroy man whom I have created from the face of the earth; both man, beast, and the creeping thing, and the fowls of the air; for it repenteth me that I have made them.
>
> And God looked upon the earth, and, behold, it was corrupt; for all flesh had corrupted his way upon the earth.

"Corrupted his way" refers to deviating from the principles that were established for the prosperity and happiness of humankind. That is to say, humankind no longer followed the laws of God, choosing instead to follow the law of the jungle.

However, God found Noah to be righteous, as revealed in Genesis 6:9: "Noah was a just man and perfect in his generations, and Noah walked with God." "Perfect" and "walked with God" indicate that Noah possessed a divine soul (was a son of God) and lived according to the "ways of God" (Noah followed the laws and divine principles). God instructed Noah to build an ark in which to place samples of life to keep seed alive upon the face of the earth. Scripture continues with the advent of the flood and the destruction of all life on earth. Genesis 7:11-12, 19-20, 23:

> In the six hundredth year of Noah's life, in the second month, the seventeenth day of the month, the same day were all the fountains of the great deep broken up, and the windows of heaven were opened. And the rain was upon the earth forty days and forty nights.
>
> And the waters prevailed exceedingly upon the earth; and all the high hills, that were under the whole heaven, were covered.
>
> And every living substance was destroyed which was upon the face of the ground, both man, and cattle, and the creeping things, and the fowl of the heaven; and they were destroyed from the earth: and Noah only remained alive, and they that were with him in the ark.

The idea of a worldwide flood that destroyed all life on earth may be viewed as biblical allegory rather than scientific fact. However, fossil and geologic discoveries indicate the earth has experienced many cataclysmic events in its history—one such event rendering the dinosaurs extinct. Thus, the biblical account of Noah's flood is not without scientific basis.

Science theorizes that the earth's surface was originally relatively smooth—possibly with "high hills" as mentioned in Genesis 7:19—and that the earth's present huge mountain ranges were formed by the colliding of the continental plates throughout earth's history. Fossilized sea life, discovered on mountain ranges, appear to support this theory. Thus, it would have been possible in the days of Noah, when the earth had not yet developed its present mountain ranges, for the surface of the earth to be completely covered by water. Science has determined that the earth's sea level would rise three hundred feet if the Arctic and Antarctic polar ice caps were to melt. Researcher Dr. Immanuel Velikovsky has written several books (*Earth in Upheaval*, etc.) that provide persuasive geological and archaeological evidence that supports the Bible's account of the flood and other cataclysmic events. Additionally, physicist Dr. James M. McCanney (e-book *Comets*) theorizes that the passage of the earth through the tail of a comet could have caused the "rain for forty days and forty nights."

The account of the flood continues in Genesis 9:18: "And the sons of Noah, that went forth of the ark, were Shem, and Ham, and Japheth: and Ham is the father of Canaan. These are the three sons of Noah: and of them was the whole earth overspread." This is the first mention of the whole earth having been populated by humankind, although it may be assumed that this was also true before the flood. This is significant because it suggests that the events within the Bible occurred on a *global scale* as substantiated by the presence of ancient megalithic structures found throughout the world. This revelation broadens the assumption that the Bible's focus is on the Middle East. The flood also demonstrates that civilization flourished when it followed the laws of God, and perished when it deviated from the laws of God.

The biblical flood reveals the importance of purity, and how the forces of nature cleanse impurity. The cleansing of impurity appears to be a natural law that allows the earth and all life to flourish. The Bible reveals that much of the world's tribulation (such as the flood) has been cleansing phenomena due to the accumulation of physical and spiritual impurities: The condition of the earth before the flood was described as "wickedness," "continual evil," and "corrupted the ways of God," which were all cleansed by the floodwaters. Thus, the earth and mankind were rejuvenated.

Our present world has accumulated many physical and spiritual impurities. The world's physical impurities appear as the pollution of the oceans, lands, and air, which threaten the earth's existence. To preserve the earth, natural cleansing phenomena such as wildfires, storms, and earthquakes are increasing to restore the earth's ability to support life.

The world's spiritual impurities (sins) appear as immorality, greed, avarice, violence, killing, stealing, dishonoring parents, wars, etc. Cleansing phenomena in the form of accidents, disease, poverty, misfortune, natural disasters, and other forms of tribulation are occurring to remove these spiritual impurities (sins). This is revealed in Revelation 7:9, 14: "I beheld, and, lo, a great multitude, which no man could number, of all nations, and kindreds, and people, and tongues, stood before the throne, and before the Lamb, clothed with white robes, and palms in their hands. These are they which came out of great tribulation, and have washed their robes, and made them white." That is to say that the stains (sins) on their robes (souls) were washed clean (atonement) by great tribulation; thus, souls were restored to their original condition (without sin) as children of God and were allowed entrance into heaven.

A serious form of physical impurity is the accumulation of toxic substances in the human body. This coincides with the proliferation of new diseases such as cancer, heart disease, kidney disease, diabetes, muscular dystrophy, attention deficit syndrome, depression, chronic fatigue, dyslexia, road rage, birth defects, etc.

Increasing knowledge about the human body reveals how the body's immune system works to preserve health by removing toxic substances. The organs of elimination that work to discharge toxins from the body include the following:

- bowel (feces, diarrhea)
- bladder (urine)
- lungs (cough, phlegm)

- sweat glands (perspiration)
- lymph glands (remove toxins from bloodstream)
- eyes (tears, pus)
- nose (mucous, poisonous blood)
- ears (pus, poisonous blood)
- skin (boils, rash, itching, pimples, blisters)

Working in tandem with the organs of elimination is the body's ability to generate heat (fever), which softens and dislodges toxins that have accumulated in various parts of the body. The released toxins are then transported through the body's circulatory system to the various organs of elimination for discharge from the body.

Through such a wondrous system, the purity of the body can be maintained and optimum health naturally occurs. The most common way that toxins are removed is called the "common cold." Although the common cold is conventionally viewed as an illness that should be treated with medicines, physicians are beginning to acknowledge the wisdom in grandmother's home remedy for treating the common cold with bed rest and soup. Hippocrates, the father of medicine, said, "Let your food be your medicine."

The Bible's account of Noah and the flood is a true record of earth's ancient history. Its narrative revealed the "principle of cleansing"—the universal law that ensures the perpetuation, regeneration, and flourishing of the earth and all life. It is important to be in harmony with this principle to achieve health, harmony, and prosperity.

A natural law of God may be paraphrased as follows: that which is full must be emptied to receive what is being given. Similarly, a soul that is filled with spiritual impurities (sins, transgressions, etc.) must be emptied (atonement) to receive the blessings of God that continually rain from heaven. Thus, prayers may seem to fall on deaf ears, and some may appear more blessed than others.

Generally speaking, there are two ways to cleanse the soul as revealed by the words of God:

1. **Passively:** "But I say unto you, Love your enemies, bless them that curse you, do good to them that hate you, and pray for them which despitefully use you, and persecute you: That ye may be the children of your Father which is in heaven" (Matthew 5:44-45).

2. **Proactively:** With a heart of apology, consider using a portion of one's time, skills, materials, etc., toward the spiritual growth of others, or toward helping to conserve what God has created.

Focusing on atonement—both passive and proactive—as part of one's spiritual training will certainly lead to the universal path of salvation. And following the way of God—not accumulating negative deeds—will leave one's soul clear to receive God's abundant blessings.

Chapter 24

God and Religion

The book of Genesis reveals that religions did not exist when mankind first populated the earth. The manner in which mankind worshipped God was simply by following "the way of God."

With the passage of time, individual languages, cultures, traditions, and beliefs came into being. This was misinterpreted as an arrangement of peoples and their gods rather than the fatherhood of God and brotherhood of man. This misunderstanding caused God to be obscured by language, culture, and the tendency to make God exclusively one's own. Thus, religions came into being.

The following is a thumbnail sketch of the origin of religions as related in scripture:

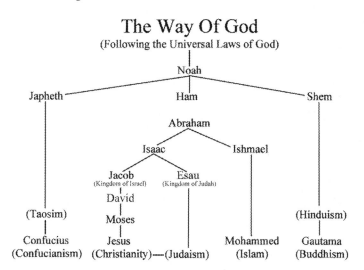

The Way Of God
(Following the Universal Laws of God)

Noah

Japheth — Ham — Shem

Abraham

Isaac — Ishmael

Jacob (Kingdom of Israel) — Esau (Kingdom of Judah)

David

(Taosim)

Moses

Confucius (Confucianism) — Jesus (Christianity) — (Judaism) — Mohammed (Islam) — Gautama (Buddhism) — (Hinduism)

The Bible reveals there is only one God, and history demonstrates that the words of God were referred to differently according to language and culture. Some cultures named the words of God after the holy messenger that conveyed them.

As man worked diligently to fulfill his service to God, he began to shift his focus toward the acquisition of personal wealth and power, thus losing sight of his true mission. To save man from engendering a hellish world, God sent holy messengers to redirect mankind toward the path of health, harmony, and prosperity. Thus, much of God's words contain guidance concerning righteous conduct. As an example, Jesus said, "Repent: for the kingdom of heaven is at hand" (Matthew 4:17).

God's messengers appeared in each religion to revive and invigorate old teachings. Their purpose was not to create new religions. However, religions—being of one origin—have served as repositories for the precious revelations of God. Therefore, all religions open their doors to anyone wishing to learn about God. This is so because deep within mankind's soul lies the memory of the fatherhood of God and the brotherhood of man.

The following are the words of God as recorded by the ancient civilizations of the Americas:

> Know ye not that there are more nations than one? Know ye not that I, the Lord your God, have created all men, and that I remember those who are upon the isles of the sea; and that I rule in the heavens above and in the earth beneath; and I bring forth my word unto the children of men, yea, even upon all the nations of the earth?

Wherefore murmur ye, because that ye shall receive more of my word? Know ye not that the testimony of two nations is a witness unto you that I am God, that I remember one nation like unto another? Wherefore, I speak the same words unto one nation like unto another. And when the two nations shall run together the testimony of the two nations shall run together also. And I do this that I may prove unto many that I am the same yesterday, today, and forever; and that I speak forth my words according to mine own pleasure.

And because that I have spoken one word ye need not suppose that I cannot speak another; for my work is not yet finished; neither shall it be until the end of man, neither from that time henceforth and forever. Wherefore, because that ye have a Bible ye need not suppose that it contains all my words; neither need ye suppose that I have not caused more to be written. For I command all men, both in the east and in the west, and in the north, and in the south, and in the islands of the sea, that they shall write the words which I speak unto them; for out of the books which shall be written I will judge the world, every man according to their works, according to that which is written. (Book of Mormon, 2 Nephi 29:7-11)

THE PARADOX OF RELIGION

Salvation by God Religious Salvation

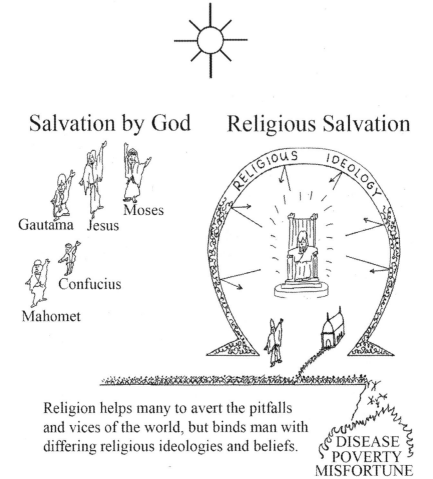

Religion helps many to avert the pitfalls
and vices of the world, but binds man with
differing religious ideologies and beliefs.

The holy saints that were sent by God to convey His Words
were all of one brotherhood. Therefore, it is odd that followers
should confront each other as religions.

Chapter 25

The Chosen People

The idea of a "chosen people" first appeared in the account of Noah and the great flood. Genesis 6:5-18 revealed God's decision to destroy all life on earth due to the continual evil and violence in the heart of mankind that caused the earth and the way of God to be corrupted. However, Noah found grace in the eyes of God because Noah was a just man, perfect in his generations, and he walked with God—that is, Noah lived his life according to the way of God. Therefore, God established a "covenant" (an agreement) with Noah to save him and his family from the great flood so they would serve as seed people for the next world age of mankind. Thus, Noah "chose" God by following the way of God, and God "chose" Noah in return because of it. This is an important point that provides insight in understanding the concept of a "chosen people."

This relationship can be seen functioning in the generations of the Bible's patriarchs—Abraham, Isaac, and Jacob (Israel). Each was found to be righteous in the eyes of God and was "chosen" by God with a covenant stating if they would faithfully maintain God's statutes and commandments, then God would bless them with prosperity and allow them to grow into mighty nations and kingdoms. Exodus 19:5-6 reveals God's reason for the covenants: "Now therefore, if ye will obey my voice indeed, and keep my covenant, then ye shall be a peculiar treasure unto me above all people. And ye shall be unto me a kingdom of priests, and an holy nation." However, Amos 3:2 reveals that being "chosen" would not absolve one's transgressions: "You only have I known of all the families of the earth: therefore I will punish you for all your iniquities." Thus, God's chosen people would suffer the same fate as others that transgressed the laws of God. This demonstrates the truism that we are all children of God, and God does not engage in favoritism.

Therefore, what might be the significance of a "chosen people"? As stated in Exodus 19:6, God's chosen would serve as "holy priests" of the world—that is, the "chosen people" are those who God has endowed with the desire and ability to nurture spiritual growth in others. They are the "keepers of sheep" referred to in Genesis 4:2, and they serve a vital role as exemplars of God's hope for mankind—without which the world would be vulnerable to unbridled greed, violence, and destruction.

Scripture reveals that the last of God's covenant/chosen people was the patriarch Jacob/Israel and his descendants, which have vanished from history as the "Lost Tribes of Israel." However, the *spirit* of God's chosen people can be seen manifesting throughout the world as expressions of love, compassion, and fairness for their fellow man. In other words, God's chosen people are those who maintain the heart of "Do unto others as ye would have others do unto you," and "Love thy neighbor as thy self." In essence, they are the workers for peace, the nonviolent, the conservers of the earth and its environment, the compassionate, and the positive, and they are among all the families of the earth. In this, the prophecy of Genesis 28:14 may be seen fulfilled: The descendants of Jacob/Israel "shall spread—as the dust of the earth—to the four corners of the earth and be a blessing to all the families of the earth."

Therefore, God's chosen people could very well be a relative, friend, neighbor, or fellow citizen. However, it is of less importance to determine whom the chosen of God are; but rather, it is vital to strive to become one who chooses God by practicing the golden rule to "Do unto others . . ." and "Love thy neighbor." Living in a manner conducive to preserving the earth and its environment would serve as an expression of filial piety toward the creation of one's Heavenly Father. This would also be a sign that one has chosen God and, in return, has been chosen by God.

Chapter 26

Jesus

The name Jesus is the English transliteration of the ancient word, *Iesu*, which may be translated as "one sent directly from the Creator/Most High God," functioning as God's spokesperson.

In John 18:37, Jesus revealed the reason for his coming: "To this end was I born, and for this cause came I into the world, that I should bear witness unto the truth. Everyone that is of the truth heareth my voice." That is, Jesus was sent to transmit the words of God to those with a spiritual relationship with God. Thus, in John 7:16 and 8:28, Jesus said, "My doctrine is not mine, but his that sent me," and "I do nothing of myself; but as my Father hath taught me, I speak these things."

Jesus's mission is further defined in Matthew 15:24: "I am not sent but unto the lost sheep of the house of Israel," and in Matthew 10:5-7 when Jesus commanded his disciples saying, "Go not into the way of the Gentiles, and into any city of the Samaritans enter ye not: But go rather to the lost sheep of the house of Israel. And as ye go, preach, saying, The kingdom of heaven is at hand."

These proclamations indicate that Jesus's mission was to fulfill God's covenant with patriarch Jacob (Israel) and his descendants, the lost sheep of Israel. Scripture does not identify the lost sheep of Israel, or where they could be found; however; in John 10:27, Jesus said, "My sheep hear my voice, and I know them, and they follow me." Thus, Jesus commanded his disciples to go forth proclaiming the words of God, knowing that those who were of God would hear and follow.

It is evident in Jesus's teachings—the words that God commanded him to speak—that it was God's wish that those of the Truth should repent (change their worldly ways) and begin following the way of God. The words of God, as proclaimed by Jesus, focused on rules of conduct as reflected in the "sermon on the mount" in Matthew 5:3-9, 38-48; 6:14-15, 19-21:

> Ye have heard that it hath been said, An eye for an eye, and a tooth for a tooth: But I say unto you, That ye resist not evil [Evil that is perpetrated against one]: but whosoever shall smite thee on thy right cheek, turn to him the other also.
>
> And if any man will sue thee at the law, and take away thy coat, let him have thy cloak also. And whosoever shall compel thee to go a mile, go with him twain.
>
> Give to him that asketh thee, and from him that would borrow of thee turn not thou away.
>
> Ye have heard that it hath been said, Thou shalt love thy neighbour, and hate thine enemy. But I say unto you, Love your enemies, bless them that curse you, do good to them that hate you, and pray for them which despitefully use you, and persecute you; That ye may be the children of your Father which is in heaven. For if ye forgive men their trespasses, your heavenly Father will also forgive you.
>
> Lay not up for yourselves treasures upon earth, where moth and rust doth corrupt, and where thieves break through and steal: But lay up for yourselves treasures in heaven, where neither moth nor rust doth corrupt, and where thieves do not break through nor steal: For where your treasure is, there will your heart be also.
>
> Blessed are the poor in spirit: for theirs is the kingdom of heaven.

> Blessed are they that mourn: for they shall be comforted.
>
> Blessed are the meek: for they shall inherit the earth.
>
> Blessed are they which do hunger and thirst after righteousness: for they shall be filled.
>
> Blessed are the merciful: for they shall obtain mercy.
>
> Blessed are the pure in heart: for they shall see God.
>
> Blessed are the peacemakers: for they shall be called the Children of God.

It can be seen that God's teachings were opposite to the way of the world, and they were truly revolutionary. Without Jesus conveying the true path to God, many would have unknowingly fallen further and further away from God. Therefore, one of Jesus's missions was to halt the widening gap separating man from God and to restore the children of God to their heavenly Father.

To extend salvation to the Gentiles (non-Israelites), Jesus appeared in a vision to Saul (Paul) of Tarsus and commanded:

> Rise, and stand upon thy feet; for I have appeared unto thee for this purpose, to make thee a minister and a witness . . . delivering thee from the people, and from the Gentiles, unto whom now I send thee, To open their eyes, and to turn them from darkness to light, and from the power of satan unto God, that they may receive forgiveness of sins, and inheritance among them which are sanctified by faith that is in me.
>
> Be of good cheer, Paul: for as thou hast testified of me in Jerusalem, so must thou bear witness also at Rome. (Acts 26:16-18; 23:11)

Thus, Paul preached the gospel in Rome, laying the foundation for the formation of the Christian religion.

Scripture reveals that Jesus was indeed one sent by God (Hebrew "Messiah," Greek "Christ") and that his mission was to warn of the impending change in God's divine plan. Jesus's teachings were meant to prepare the children of God for the approaching kingdom of heaven through repentance—that is, to change from the way of the world and to begin living according to the laws of heaven. The role to gather the lost sheep of Israel and to rule over the house of Israel as king would be fulfilled during Jesus's Second Coming as the promised Messiah of the Old Testament.

Chapter 27

The Promised Messiah

"Messiah" is from the Old Testament Hebrew *mashahh*, which means "anointed," or one chosen or sent from God. The New Testament Greek equivalent is *khristos* or "Christ."

Many men have been described as being "anointed" in Hebrew scripture. The Israelite kings David, Saul, and Solomon and the patriarchs Abraham, Isaac, and Jacob were anointed ones. Although not mentioned as being "anointed," Enos (Genesis 4:26: "then began men to call upon the name of the Lord"), Noah (chosen to preserve seed for life after the flood), and Moses (preserved and guided the tribes of Israel) were obviously chosen by God, or anointed ones. The most celebrated anointed one (Messiah or Christ) was Jesus. Thus, an anointed one may be considered one that has been chosen by God for a specific role.

The term "promised Messiah" is understood to refer to an anointed one that would one day appear (scripture infers the end-times) to restore the house of Israel and establish its rightful place in the world. This savior would also establish the house of God and usher in the kingdom of heaven on earth.

Early references in the Old Testament to a "promised one" were vague and obscure and often appeared as part of prophesies. For example, Genesis 49:10: "The scepter shall not depart from Judah, nor a lawgiver from between his feet, until Shiloh come; and unto him shall the gathering of the people be." Also, Deuteronomy 18:18: "I will raise them up a Prophet from among their brethren, like unto thee [Moses], and will put my words in his mouth; and he shall speak unto them all that I shall command him." And Micah 5:2: "But thou, Bethlehem Ephratah, though thou be little among the thousands of Judah, yet out of thee shall he come forth unto me that is to be ruler in Israel."

Such prophetic statements provided enough information to create anticipation among the lost sheep of Israel for the savior that would ultimately appear in their behalf. However, the vagueness of the prophecies caused great confusion during the appearance of Jesus. The humble appearance of Jesus arriving on a pack animal seemed to contradict the expectation of a Messiah that would triumphantly arrive as the king of the Israelites. Hence, there was great debate among the multitude and certain religious leaders. Although Jesus's words and miracles testified of one sent by God, he was severely judged for his humanness and was rejected and ridiculed. Also, the words of Jesus were perceived as a threat to the established religion that had lost its spirituality since the days of Moses. As a result, the men of religion (Scribes, Pharisees, and Sadducees)—fearing an erosion of their authority—conspired against Jesus. However, some people recognized the voice of God in Jesus's sermons and followed him.

The background of the promised Messiah—being from the tribe of Judah, a descendant of David, the shepherd of Israel—clearly applies to Jesus. Also, the teachings and works of Jesus indicate that he was indeed a Messiah (anointed one) who was sent by God. However, it can also be seen that Jesus's mission at that time was not that of the "promised Messiah" who would appear during the end-times to reestablish the house of Israel and construct the temple of the Lord. Jesus's mission—as revealed in Matthew 4:17: "From that time Jesus began to preach, and to say, Repent: for the kingdom of heaven is at hand"—was to warn people of the impending change in God's divine plan (the coming kingdom of heaven) and to prepare people by guiding them back to righteousness.

The role of the "promised Messiah" would be fulfilled during Jesus's Second Coming as the Son of man. It will be during the time of his Second Coming that the Son of man will fulfill all that has been prophesied about the promised Messiah. Thus, the children of God—scattered as the dew on the earth—all await the savior that has promised to return, which scripture refers to as "the Second Coming."

Chapter 28

The Second Coming

?

The following Old Testament prophecy from the book of Isaiah presents a broad view for the idea of a promised Messiah and a Second Coming.

Isaiah 10:10: "And in that day there shall be a root [Jesus] of Jesse [Ise, the seat of the Cherubim], which shall stand for an ensign of the people [the lost sheep of Israel]; to it shall the Gentiles [non-Israelites] seek: and his rest [Jesus's ascension to heaven] shall be glorious."

Isaiah 10:11: "And it shall come to pass in that day [the end-times], that the Lord shall set his hand again the second time [the Second Coming/promised Messiah] to recover the remnant of his people."

Isaiah 10:12: "And he shall set up an ensign [the house of the Lord] for the nations, and shall assemble the outcasts of Israel, and gather together the dispersed of Judah [the lost sheep] from the four corners of the earth."

In various chapters of the New Testament, Jesus revealed to his disciples that he (the Son of man) would be returning during a later period (the end-times). The anticipation of Jesus's return has been termed the "Second Coming." Jesus frequently referred to his returning as the coming of the Son of man. It appears he did so to alert his disciples that he would not be returning as the historical Jesus with which his disciples and the world were familiar.

In Matthew 24:23, 26-27, Jesus revealed key points concerning his Second Coming: "Then if any man shall say unto you, Lo, here is Christ, or there; believe it not." This is to say that the Son of man (Jesus) *would not be returning as the Jesus Christ of two thousand years ago.* "Wherefore if they shall say unto you, Behold, he is in the desert; go not forth; behold, he is in the secret chambers; believe it not." This is to say that he would not be appearing in the desert (Middle East). Nor would he be a member of a secret society. "For as the lightning cometh out of the east, and shineth even unto the west; so shall also the coming of the Son of man be." This is to say that the Son of man will be appearing in a country in the East, from which the light has emanated since time immemorial (i.e., the land of the Cherubim, and he will travel to the West). (There are many native traditions and folklore that speak of a messiah-like figure that brought them the way of civilization and righteous behavior [the tree of life] with the promise to one-day return.)

In Matthew 24:3, 6-8, 30, Jesus revealed the signs heralding the end of the world and the coming of the Son of man:

> And as he sat upon the mount of Olives, the disciples came unto him privately, saying, Tell us, when shall these things be? And what shall be the sign of thy coming, and of the end of the world?
>
> And ye shall hear of wars and rumors of wars: see that ye be not troubled: for all these things must come to past, but the end is not yet. For nation shall rise against nation, and kingdom against kingdom: and there shall be famines, and pestilences, and earthquakes, in diverse places. All these are the beginning of sorrows.
>
> And then shall appear the sign of the Son of man in heaven . . . and they shall see the Son of man coming in the clouds of heaven with power and great glory.

These verses reveal that the Son of man—Jesus/the Second Coming—shall appear during a time of increasing tribulation on earth. The period of "wars and rumors of wars . . . nation shall rise against nation . . . famines, and pestilences, and earthquakes, in diverse places" is applicable to the world's recent history. "All these are the beginnings of sorrows" would indicate events that precede the book of Revelation's "end of the world." Thus, the Son of man shall appear during the period of tribulation to fulfill all that has been prophesied in scripture: he shall gather the lost sheep of Israel, restore the temple of the house of the Lord, reestablish the Holy Place with the ark of the covenant as was in the days of Moses, and again bring "baptism by fire and Holy Spirit" into the world to seal "the servants of our God in their foreheads" (Revelation 7:3).

Revelation 22:13 states: "I am Alpha and Omega, the beginning and the end, the first and the last." That is to say that Jesus has been in the world since the very beginning, and he will be in the world again when the world finally ends. Thus, it can be seen that the great Holy Spirit—who sits on the right of power—has appeared in the world on numerous occasions, the most notable being his appearance two thousand years ago as Jesus. This Great

Spirit (scripture often refers to him as the Son of man) will appear again as the promised Messiah during the Second Coming.

The Son of man appeared two thousand years ago as a man named Jesus, to walk and talk among humans. When the Son of man appears during the Second Coming, he will again be born as a human being, to walk and talk among humans. This is referred to in Revelation 7:2: "And I saw another angel ascending from the east, having the seal of the living God." "Ascending," to slowly rise, indicates being born and raised in a country in the East. "Having the seal of the living God," indicates that the Son of man (promised Messiah) will not be a member of any established religion. Rather, he will again be the conveyor of the words of the true, living God—the creator of heaven and earth. The "seal" would ostensibly be related to the Star of David (the seal of Moses, David, and Jesus), possibly combined with the seal of the Cherubim (God's original representatives on earth). This would indicate that the promised Messiah was sent as a representative of the true living God and not from any of the world's religions. The following is a rendition of what the seal of the living God may possibly appear as:

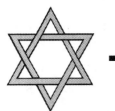 +  =

| The Seal of Moses David and Jesus | Cherubim Seal Behind Christ | The Seal of the Promised Messiah? |

The means of travel during the time of Jesus was by walking, by domesticated animals, and by seagoing vessels. The means of travel during our modern age are the automobile, train, seagoing vessel, and aircraft. Thus, when the Son of man (promised Messiah) travels from the East to the West, he will be traveling either by seagoing vessel or aircraft. "And they shall see the Son of man coming in the clouds of heaven with power and great glory" (Matthew 24:30) would indicate traveling to the West by aircraft.

The following are biblical passages that help define the appearance of the Son of man:

Matthew 24:37, 38, 44: "But as in the days of Noe were . . . eating, drinking, marrying . . . so shall also the coming of the Son of man be. Therefore, be ye also ready: for in such an hour as ye think not the Son of man cometh." The Son of man will appear at a time when people will be going about their lives in the typical manner of the day, and most shall be unaware of his presence.

Thessalonians 5:2: "For yourselves know perfectly that the day of the Lord so cometh as a thief in the night." When a thief appears in the night, only those who the thief has visited will have knowledge of his coming. Others, who have not been visited, may say that the thief is yet to come. This is to say that the world shall be unaware of the appearance of the Son of man because the circumstances of his appearance will not meet preconceived expectations. This would be similar to events two thousand years ago when Jesus appeared and went unrecognized. Know that if a thief has not visited, it does not necessarily follow that the thief is yet to come.

In John 14:3, Jesus confides in his disciples: "I will come again and receive you unto myself; that where I am, there ye may be also." This reveals that when the Son of man appears at the Second Coming, so also shall his disciples be gathered to him.

John 16:25: "These things have I spoken unto you in proverbs: but the time cometh when I shall no more speak unto you in proverbs, but I shall show you plainly of the Father." The Son of man will reveal the mysteries of God to his disciples at the time of the Second Coming.

Micah 4:1-2: "But in the last days it shall come to pass, that the mountain of the house of the Lord shall be established in the top of the mountains [Japan Alps?], and it shall be exalted above the hills; and people shall flow unto it. And many nations shall come, and say, Come, and let us go up to the mountain of the Lord, and to the house of the God of Jacob; and he will teach us of his ways, and we will walk in his paths: for the law shall go forth of Zion [God's land/land of the gods], and the word of the Lord from Jerusalem [holy city/place of the Cherubim and the Son of man]."

The Bible indicates that there was great expectation for the appearance of Jesus; however, when Jesus did not meet preconceived notions, he was rejected as not being the one sent from God. Scripture—Matthew 17:12: "But I say unto you, That Elias is come already, and they knew him not, but have done unto him whatsoever they listed. Likewise shall also the Son of man suffer of them"—suggests that a similar rejection may occur with the appearance of the promised Messiah/Second Coming of Jesus.

An article in the December 24, 1979, issue of *Newsweek* magazine titled, "The Faces of Jesus," relates how the perception of Jesus has changed throughout history. To illustrate, the article presented four pictures of Jesus from various parts of the world: A Grunewald painting showed the crucified Jesus with Germanic features. A Byzantine mosaic rendered Jesus with a strong Middle Eastern ethnicity. A painting by Rembrandt portrayed Jesus in the clothes and posture of a sixteenth-century European aristocrat. And a modern image portrayed Jesus as the romanticized, handsome image reminiscent of Hollywood.

The *Newsweek* article begs the question, "Which Son of man/ Jesus will the world expect to see during the Second Coming?"

Chapter 29

Baptism by Fire and Holy Spirit

Jesus baptizing an infant with "Fire and Holy Spirit"

In Matthew 3:11, John the Baptist proclaimed, "I indeed baptize you with water unto repentance: but he that cometh after me is mightier than I, whose shoes I am not worthy to bear: he shall baptize you with the Holy Ghost, and with fire."

Jesus was granted the power to baptize (to purify the spirit) with fire (God's power) radiated from the palm of the hand. Jesus is often depicted "baptizing with fire" by radiating the power of God to the forehead. Revelation 7:3 refers to this as "sealed the servants of our God in their forehead." The power to baptize with fire was a sign of one sent directly from God.

Moses was also granted God's power. This was recorded in Exodus 17:9, 11-13, when Israel battled the Amalekites in Rephidim: "And Moses said unto Joshua, Choose us out men, and go out, fight with Amalek: tomorrow I will stand on the top of the hill with the rod of God in mine hand. And it came to pass, when Moses held up his hand, that Israel prevailed: and when he let down his hand, Amalek prevailed. But Moses' hands were heavy, and they took a stone, and put it under him, and he sat thereon; and Aaron and Hur stayed up his hands, the one on the one side, and the other on the other side; and his hands were steady until the going down of the sun. And Joshua discomfited Amalek and his people with the edge of the sword."

Moses directing God's power to the Israelites

Jesus granted the power to baptize with fire to his disciples, and in Matthew 10:8, commanded them, saying, "Heal the sick, cleanse the lepers, raise the dead, cast out devils; freely ye have received, freely give." That is, the disciples had been granted God's power and were commanded to freely give it to others.

"Baptism by fire and Holy Spirit" meant to be spiritually purified by the light of God and Jesus. However, during the end-times, "baptism by fire" will also represent the purification of the world through the great tribulation—a momentous time of wars, famines, and natural and man-made disasters.

Revelation 7:2-3 reveals that the end-times will also be a time when God will display great mercy by providing salvation through his promised Messiah/Second Coming: "And I saw another angel [promised Messiah] ascending from the east, having the seal of the living God: and he cried with a loud voice to the four angels, to whom it was given to hurt the earth and sea, Saying, Hurt not the earth, neither the sea, nor the trees, till we have sealed the servants of our God in their foreheads." Thus, as God purifies the earth, the world will have a choice to be purified by tribulation or by the promised Messiah. Therefore, receiving the light of God in the forehead ("sealed . . . in their foreheads") will be a source of divine protection and salvation during the great tribulation.

Science (Dr. Daniel Amen/*Change Your Brain, Change Your Life*) has ascertained that the area of the forehead called the prefrontal cortex of the brain is the source of human consciousness. It represents 30 percent of the brain's activity in humans, versus only 11 percent in chimpanzees and 7 percent in dogs. This data demonstrates the important role that the area of the forehead plays in human consciousness and development.

Religion refers to the forehead area as the "third eye" or "spiritual eye"—a source of enlightenment and connection with God. Situated deeper within the forehead, near the center of the brain, lies the pineal gland. Science has discovered that the pineal gland contains minute crystalline granules ("acervuli," or "brain sand") of undetermined function. The fact that crystals have the ability to resonate with invisible emanations—such as radio signals received by crystal radio sets of old—suggests that the pineal gland may serve as a receptor for emanations from

God. It is of interest to note that classical scientist/philosopher Rene Descartes referred to the pineal gland as the "seat of the soul." Thus, it would appear that God's power administered to the forehead would have the effect of purifying the soul (i.e., purifying/removing sins as well as the suffering associated with those sins). Hence, when Jesus baptized with "fire and holy spirit," it is written in Matthew 9:6: "But that ye may know that the Son of Man hath power on earth to forgive sins."

These data suggest a scientific basis for understanding why Jesus radiated the power of God to the area of the forehead: the power of God in the forehead would revive the capacity to spiritually awaken, feel reverence, reflect, and repent—such capacities being diminished by the "way of the world." The power of God directed to the pineal gland would strengthen one's spiritual connection with God. This is to say that "the art of baptism by fire" is a means to grow spiritually and become Christlike.

Two thousand years ago, the art of baptism by fire and Holy Spirit made a brief appearance in the world with Jesus and his disciples. When the art of baptism by fire and Holy Spirit is again seen in the world, know that the Son of man and his disciples have appeared to again offer salvation to the world.

In reference to his Second Coming, Jesus foretold the exploits of his disciples in Matthew 24:28: "For wheresoever the carcass [those experiencing great tribulation] is, there will the eagles [disciples] be gathered together" (giving salvation by baptizing with fire and Holy Spirit—that is, offering the light of God to others). Also, in Matthew 14:13, Jesus revealed, "The works that I do shall ye do also; and greater works than these shall ye do."

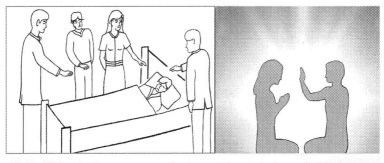

Disciples Transmitting The Light of God

Know that with the appearance of the Son of man/Second Coming shall be the appearance of baptism by fire and Holy Spirit. (An authoritative source on baptism by fire [spiritual purification] is *Mahikari—Thank God for the Answers At Last*, by Dr. A. K. Tebecis.)

Chapter 30

The Holy Place

The book of Exodus, chapters 25 through 30, describes how God instructed Moses to construct a sanctuary so God may "dwell among the congregation." God's sanctuary consisted of the tabernacle of the congregation and a holy altar upon which prayers and burnt offerings would be offered. It is in this sanctuary that God would speak with Moses and meet with the children of Israel.

In addition, Moses was instructed to make a "laver of brass to wash withal," which should be placed between the tabernacle of the congregation and the altar. Thereat, Aaron and his sons should wash their hands and their feet when they go into the tabernacle of the congregation or when they approached the altar to minister. Exodus 30:21: "So they shall wash their hands and their feet, that they die not: and it shall be a statute for ever to them, even to him and to his seed throughout their generations."

The sanctuary would serve as a contact point where man could meet God face-to-face. Therefore, they were instructed to "wash their hands and their feet"—in modern times, maintaining cleanliness of the feet would be accomplished by the use of clean foot covering, such as socks, hosiery, etc.—to maintain purity. In Exodus 26:33, 28:43, and 39:1, God referred to this sanctuary as "the holy place."

In Matthew 24:15, Jesus spoke privately with his disciples about his Second Coming and the end of the world: "When ye therefore shall see the abomination of desolation [the great tribulation] spoken of by Daniel the prophet, stand in the holy place, [whoso readeth, let him understand]." This reveals that the "holy place" would be in existence during the end-times, and it would be a place of divine protection and salvation.

Revelation 7:2 reveals that the Son of man (Second Coming) would appear bearing the seal of the living God. "Living God" indicates being the bearer of truth and not affiliated with existing religions. Therefore, the reestablishment of the "holy place" and its statutes, spoken of by Daniel the prophet, would herald the appearance of the Son of man—the long-awaited promised Messiah.

Chapter 31

The Holy Spirit

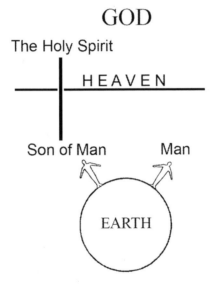

GOD

The Holy Spirit

HEAVEN

Son of Man   Man

EARTH

The Holy Spirit appears unique to the Bible's New Testament. Jesus used the term while consoling his disciples during his farewell. The following scripture contains key points concerning Jesus's use of the term "the Holy Spirit."

In John 14:26, Jesus states, "the Comforter, which is the Holy Spirit." In this verse, Jesus identifies the Comforter and the Holy Spirit as one and the same.

In John 14:16, Jesus states, "And I will pray the Father, and he shall give you another Comforter." "*Another* Comforter" indicates that the disciples already have a comforter in Jesus. This defines a "comforter" as being like Jesus—someone who comes from heaven to walk among men and who serves as master to his disciples.

In John 14:18, Jesus states, "I will not leave you comfortless: I will come to you." "I will not leave you comfortless" restates Jesus's promise that his disciples will be provided with another comforter. "I will come to you," says that it will be Jesus who will be returning as the promised comforter. This is a reference to the Second Coming/Son of man.

In John 14:26, Jesus states, "But the Comforter, which is The Holy Spirit, whom the Father will send in my name, he shall teach you all things and bring all things to your remembrance, whatsoever I have said unto you." "But the Comforter, which is The Holy Spirit, whom the Father will send in my name" indicates that the Comforter/Holy Spirit/Jesus will be returning to earth (the Second Coming). "He shall teach you all things and bring all things to your remembrance, whatsoever I have said unto you" indicates that the "Comforter/Holy Spirit/Jesus/Second Coming" will reunite with his disciples and reveal to them their past relationship. This is also referenced in John 14:3, "I will come again, and receive you unto myself; that where I am, there ye may be also."

In summary, the verses in chapter 14 of the book of John reveal the following:

"The Holy Spirit" is he who sits on the right of God. From "Alpha to Omega" he has appeared on earth, being born of woman, to walk among men to fulfill God's will.

The Holy Spirit's name is not known to anyone on earth; thus, he is often referred to as the Son of man. His most noted appearance was as Jesus—it is the most noted because a world religion was formed as a result of his divine service.

Jesus's disciples have only one master, and that master is Jesus. Jesus's use of the term, "comforter," is indicative of a very personal relationship between a master and his disciples. Thus, Jesus would reassure his disciples that they would not be without a master (comforter), and he "would pray the Father, and he shall give you another Comforter." This is a reference to the reuniting of master and disciples during Jesus's Second Coming, and they would again convey the words of God, just as they did in the past.

Chapter 32

The Beast 666

"Here is wisdom. Let him that hath understanding count the number of the beast: for it is the number of a man; and his number is six hundred three score and six" (Revelation 13:18).

In the ancient language, the numeral six was represented by a pictograph of a man standing. Six also represented the six parts of man: four limbs, a body and a head. Thus, the numeral six is strongly related to the physical aspect of man. The combination of 6-6-6 suggests an individual (spirit, mind, and body) that is spiritually bound to the earth (i.e., 666 represents earthly man).

The first mention of earthly man appears in Genesis 4:1: "And Adam knew Eve his wife; and she conceived, and bare Cain, and said, I have gotten a man from the Lord." "Gotten a man from the Lord" reveals that the firstborn Cain represented earthly or worldly man. Cain is described as a "tiller of the ground" whose descendants were builders of cities, those who dwelt in tents and raised cattle, fathers of those who handle the harp and organ, and artificers in brass and iron. In other words, Cain represented those endowed with the desire and ability to develop the wealth of the earth (i.e., men of industry who were given the role to "subdue the earth" or develop civilization as mentioned in Genesis 1:28). In a fit of wrath Cain killed his brother Abel, and when asked of his brother's whereabouts replied, "Am I my brother's keeper?" This reveals that the nature of earthly man is to focus on material development with little regard for anything else.

Cain was the first to commit murder in the world and feared retribution: "And I shall be a fugitive and a vagabond in the earth; and it shall come to pass, that every one that findeth me shall slay me. And the Lord said unto him, Therefore whosoever slayeth Cain, vengeance shall be taken on him sevenfold. And the Lord set a mark upon Cain, lest any finding him should kill him" (Genesis 4:14-15). Scripture does not elucidate about that mark; however, it may be significant because of a possible relationship with "the mark of the beast" mentioned in the book of Revelation.

The term, "the beast," gained notoriety in the end-time prophecies in the book of Daniel and the book of Revelation. "The beast" refers to man that lives according to the law of the jungle (i.e., the way of the world in which "might makes right," "money talks," and "the end justifies the means" is the rule).

The law of the jungle is opposite to the law of God, which may be paraphrased as the law of "Do unto others as you would have others do unto you," and "Love thy neighbor as thy self." Individuals that live their lives according to the law of God are referred to in scripture as the "children of God." Individuals that live their lives according to the law of the jungle are referred to as "man the beast."

The God-given role of man is embodied in the symbol of the Sphinx. The Sphinx lies at the foot of the pyramid (God's holy altar), revealing it to be an emissary of God. The Sphinx's human head represents a child of god. The body of a lion represents its noble embodiment—that is, a child of God appearing as ruler in a beastly world of violence and survival of the fittest. However, the Sphinx may also reflect the present condition of mankind (i.e., man has *become* a beast that only wears the mask of a human face).

The gaze of the Sphinx is focused outward toward the world, indicating the area of its mission. Thus, the Sphinx and the pyramid symbolize the important role given to mankind: Man was granted dominion of the earth and all its creatures with the command to go forth and subdue it—that is, to make the earth a civilized place where the tree of life may flourish and provide sustenance for mankind's quest to become divine in character.

However, mankind's history—from the very beginning when Cain slew Abel—has been characterized by violence and "man's inhumanity to man." This was prophesied in a vision by the prophet Daniel: "And four great beasts came up from the sea, divers one from another" (Daniel 7:3). That is, four ages of man would follow, each characterized by violence (the law of the jungle). This suggests that the "law of the jungle" is synonymous with "the way of the world."

"The way of the world" (survival of the fittest) represents a reality in which mankind had to function when cast from the Garden of Eden. Thus, to carry out God's command to "subdue the earth," man had to survive by using violence to fend off aggressors, hunt for food, etc.—much like it is to this day. Therefore, it need not be supposed that the "beast/666" should necessarily be diabolical in nature. Rather, "the beast/666" could very well be a beloved leader of a mighty nation that uses its military might to accomplish its goals.

World ages or civilizations that function under the law of the jungle have been described collectively as "the beast." The term "the beast" has also been used to refer to a specific individual as described in Revelation 13:18: "Here is wisdom. Let him that hath understanding count the number of the beast: for it is the number of a man: and his number is Six hundred threescore and six." This reveals that 666 is the number of a specific individual who epitomizes the way of the world (man-the-beast). Revelation 13:17 states: "The name of the beast, or the number of his name." This infers that the number of letters in a first, middle, and last name equal 6-6-6. That individual—with the role to develop the wealth of the earth—is also referred to in scripture as the Antichrist.

Chapter 33

The Antichrist

In the beginning, God brought forth the firstborn Cain, a "tiller of the soil" endowed with desire for material wealth, whose mission was to develop the wealth of the earth. Then God brought forth the second-born, Abel, a "keeper of sheep" endowed with desire to be his brother's keeper, whose mission was to nurture humankind's spirituality. Cain and Abel were archetypes representing two sides of a coin. They were the original "soul mates" or counterparts that God created to maintain balance in humankind. It would appear that it was God's will that Cain and Abel and their descendants should use their God-given talents to work for the progress of humankind. The Son of man (the Good Shepherd/Christ) and his counterpart (the Antichrist) represent the embodiment of both archetypes of humankind.

The Bible reveals that when the age of man comes to an end, the Son of man and his counterpart shall both be present, each fulfilling their God-given missions. The Son of man shall work toward the *spiritual* development of humankind, and the Antichrist shall work toward developing the *material* wealth of the earth.

Christ's counterpart has often been portrayed as an evil dictator—perhaps even satanic—with intent to enslave the world. This portrayal may be somewhat off-the-mark. Christ's counterpart (the Antichrist) could very well be a beloved leader of a great nation who strives for economic prosperity.

Revelation 13:5 describes the beast (Antichrist and/or world power) as "was unto him given a mouth speaking great things and blasphemies." "A mouth speaking great things" suggests that the Antichrist/world power would be a gifted speaker using the power of global communication to spread the promise of material wealth and prosperity. "Speaking . . . blasphemies" may mean that the Antichrist or powerful nation would associate himself/itself with God and righteousness.

The term "Antichrist" refers to that which is the opposite of Christ. Christ nurtured spiritual development though expressions of love. The opposite of love is war. This suggests that the Antichrist would be a proponent of war. War and the use of military power ("might makes right" and "the end justifies the means") would be the method used to achieve material wealth and economic prosperity.

Receiving the "mark of the beast in the forehead or right hand" (Revelation 13:16) appears related to one's innermost attitude and deeds. If one unknowingly accepts the law of the jungle ("might makes right," etc.) and lives his or her life according to it, it can be said that one has received the "mark of the beast" in their forehead (their way of thinking) and in their right hand (their way of living). "That no man might buy or sell, save he that had the mark, or the name of the beast, or the number of his name" (Revelation 13:17) implies that people or nations must become like-minded to partake in material prosperity.

There has been much interest and speculation that focuses on a physical "mark" and what that mark may actually be. Some have suggested that it may be akin to an identification number, such as a Social Security number. Others believe it to be something more sinister, such as a computer chip that may be imbedded under the skin. And, many believe that the mass use of vaccinations qualifies as a form of the "mark of the beast." These speculations reflect a keen interest in people's desire to avoid receiving a mark that would associate them with the Antichrist. However, scripture reveals that God places priority on what is truly in one's heart rather than what may be on one's physical body.

The Bible's message is focused on the spiritual development of a "loving heart" by following the principle of "do unto others as you would have others do unto you" and "love thy neighbor as thy self." A "loving heart" is the sign of a child of God, regardless of any physical "mark." This is a key point that can easily be lost when nation is set against nation and when "thy neighbor" is characterized as "the enemy." Under such conditions, a charismatic leader may persuade many to beat the drums of war.

The Bible also speaks of receiving the seal of God in one's forehead or right hand as the alternative to receiving the mark of the beast. Scripture (Revelation 7:2) reveals that the "seal of God in one's forehead" will be given by the Son of man/promised Messiah/Second Coming through baptism by fire and Holy Spirit—that is, radiating the light of God from the palm of the hand to the forehead. This will be the method of salvation that leads to returning to be a child of God.

Very few people have the capacity to serve in leadership roles. Even fewer have the capacity to function in the world arena. For those who lack courage, strength, or desire to serve in such an arena, a great debt of gratitude is owed to those who do serve. The world should pray that those with the role to "develop the wealth of the earth" could accomplish their mission in a way that would cause less suffering for others, and in a way that would not defile the earth, nor cause God to cleanse the world as was done in the days of Noah.

All the blessings of our modern age are due to the "blood, sweat and tears" of those who have courageously fulfilled their God-given mission to "develop the wealth of the earth." The technological/informational age of today would not have been possible without their great effort and sacrifices—nor would it be possible for the words of God/true history of the world/revelations of the Son of man to be disseminated throughout the world. Thus, both Christ and the Antichrist serve to fulfill God's will.

Chapter 34

The Lost Tribes of Israel

The mystery of the lost tribes of Israel begins in the Garden of Eden in Genesis 2:10: "And a river went out of Eden to water the garden; and from thence it was parted, and became into four heads."

"And a river went out of Eden" signifies the emergence of *mankind's civilizations* from the Garden of Eden. "And became into four heads" indicates mankind's civilizations manifesting as *four world ages*—each world age ending by cataclysms of nature (e.g., mankind's first world age ended with the great flood of Noah). The "four heads" (world ages) coincide with the *Bible's four patriarchs*: Noah, Abraham, Isaac, and Jacob (Israel).

Scripture often refers to the patriarchs as individual people to more clearly convey historical events. However, in other instances, the patriarchs are referred to as peoples, nations, and kingdoms, indicating that they were the principals of a particular world age.

Thus, the biblical account of patriarchs Noah, Abraham, Isaac, and Jacob would be a record of God's covenant people being the principals during mankind's first (Noah), second (Abraham), third (Isaac), and fourth (Jacob/Israel) world ages, respectively—all world ages having originated in the Garden of Eden.

In many instances, scripture states simply that Abraham begot Isaac, and Isaac begot Jacob, to make plain the passage of the scepter from one patriarch (world age) to another—without disclosing the catastrophic events that occurred between generations. Thus, the ending of the kingdom of Israel would represent the ending of the fourth world age and the restructuring of the earth and its people. The survivors of such a catastrophic event would have been thrown back to a primitive existence, and memories of their previous world would have been recorded for posterity written on stone or clay tablets or immortalized in song, chants, and folklore.

The ancient records of mankind, preserved in India and translated by the late Col. James Churchward (*The Lost Continent of Mu* and other books), revealed the existence of a wondrous land called Mu, the Motherland of Man (the Bible's Garden of Eden), that occupied a vast area of the South Pacific. These records, preserved on ancient clay tablets, contained precious knowledge concerning mankind's ultra-ancient beginnings, the history of mankind's expansion throughout the earth, and the story of Mu's sad ending. These records revealed that Mu's sixty-four million inhabitants, having reached the height of material development, fell from righteousness and caused their kingdom to be destroyed by tremendous earthquakes and volcanic eruptions, being "rent asunder" and sinking into the abyss of the Pacific Ocean—its remnant being Japan and the islands of the Pacific.

It is of interest that the Japanese call their country "Nihon," which translates to "the land of sun" (the light that shines from the East). According to the ancient records written in the book *Ohaspe*, the modern name "Japan" is derived from the ancient word "Zah Pan," which translates to "the relic of Pan." Pan, a name familiar to the Greek philosopher Plato, was a name for the continent of Mu before its final destruction.

Of equal interest is a July 4, 2011, Reuters news story on the discovery by a team from Japan, led by Yasuhiro Kato, an associate professor from the University of Tokyo Graduate School of Engineering, of vast amounts of mineral-rich mud (*soil*) found on the ocean floor in the central and southeastern regions of the Pacific Ocean. The convulsions that destroyed the continent of Mu would have certainly turned that area of the Pacific into a sea of mud. Could the recently discovered mineral-rich mud be the residue of the legendary Mu continent (Garden of Eden)?

Genesis 2:10 revealed that the Garden of Eden would be the source of "four heads," or world ages of mankind. Further biblical references to these four world ages are sparse and indirect at best. However, the ancient records of the Native American Hopi reveal that the Garden of Eden sank beneath the sea at the end of the fourth world age. This supports the biblical revelation that the Garden of Eden would be the source of only four world ages. The ancient records from India link the Bible's Garden of Eden with the continent of Mu ("Motherland of Man"), which was situated in the middle of the Pacific Ocean.

The Old Testament's historical narrative appears to end with the destruction of the kingdom of Israel and the dispersing of its people, signaling the end of the Bible's last patriarch, Jacob/Israel. I believe it would be safe to conclude that the ancient records of man—the Bible's Old Testament, the records of the Hopi, and the records of the Mu continent—identify the Garden of Eden, the continent of Mu and the kingdom of Israel as being one and the same. It is of keen interest that the star of David—the seal of Moses, King David, Jesus, and the ancient kingdom of Israel—held a position of preeminence among the sacred symbols from the continent of Mu.

Genesis 28:14 states, in God's guidance to Jacob (Israel), "And thy seed shall be as the dust of the earth, and thou shalt spread abroad to the west, and to the east, and to the north, and to the south: and in thee and in thy seed shall all the families of the earth be blessed." Therefore, should the kingdom of Israel represent the last world age to emerge from the Garden of Eden (the Mu continent in the Pacific Ocean), then its inhabitants would have "spread abroad to the west" to the continents of North and South America (Native Americans, Mayans, Aztecs, Incas, etc.), "and to the east" to Asia and the Orient (Japanese, Chinese, Koreans and other related oriental races), "and to the north" (the Ainu, Eskimos, and Native Americans), "and to the south" (aboriginal and related Pacific Islanders). It would be more than a coincidence that all of these people share a common creation story, a common understanding of a divine hierarchy and supreme Creator, a common gift of spirituality, and the common physical characteristic of being "smooth skinned" people (Genesis 27:11: "And Jacob [Israel] said to Rebekah his mother, Behold, Esau my brother is a hairy man, and I am a smooth man").

These cultural similarities may also explain why "Jomon-style" ceramic and other artifacts indigenous to Japan should be found in archaeological sites on the West Coast of North America, and why the majority of the world's oldest pyramidal and ceremonial stone structures should be situated in lands bordering the Pacific Ocean—or, as in the megalithic structure discovered near Yonaguni-Jima, Japan, submerged beneath the sea.

Another similarity among peoples of the Pacific is the sharing of a common language or etymology. The languages of the lesser islands of the Pacific, being situated near major landmasses, reflect the influence of other cultures. However, the aboriginal people of the Hawaiian Islands—being virtually isolated in the middle of the Pacific Ocean—have maintained a language that has been least affected by change.

A cursory look at the Hawaiian language provides insight to its origin. The Hawaiian language is based on an alphabet of twelve letters—five vowels (*a, i, u, e, o*) and seven consonants (*w, l, m, h, n, p, k*)—that combine to form a forty-character syllabary from which words are formed. To illustrate, the twelve-letter alphabet may be placed on a matrix with seven consonants on the horizontal axis and five vowels on the vertical axis, resulting in a chart showing all possible syllabic permutations of vowels and consonants. By combining the "a," "lo" and "ha" syllables, the famous Hawaiian word aloha is formed. When viewed in matrix form, it becomes readily apparent that the Hawaiian syllabary is nearly identical to the ancient Japanese Katakana syllabary. The following graphic illustrates this point.

	(R)			(T)						
W	L	M	H	N	P		K			— CONSONANTS
wa	la	ma	ha	na	pa		ka	a	A	
wi	li	mi	hi	ni	pi		ki	i	I	
wu	lu	mu	hu	nu	pu		ku	u	U	—VOWELS
we	le	me	he	ne	pe		ke	e	E	
wo	lo	mo	ho	no	po		ko	o	O	

The Hawaiian Alphabet and Syllabary

	(L)				(P)					
W	R	Y	M	H	N	T	S	K	a	A
wa	ra	ya	ma	ha	na	ta	sa	ka	a	A
i	ri	i	mi	hi	ni	chi	si	ki	i	I
u	ru	yu	mu	hu	nu	tsu	su	ku	u	U
e	re	e	me	he	ne	te	se	ke	e	E
n	wo	ro	yo	mo	ho	no	to	so	ko	o	O

The Japanese Katakana Syllabary

A comparison of the two matrices strongly suggests that the Hawaiian syllabary is related to the ancient Japanese syllabary. It is possible that the ancient Hawaiian language, originally a spoken language, may have discontinued the use of its *y* and *s* sounds over millennia. The Hawaiian *l* is often interchanged with the Katakana *r* in modern use. Also, possibly the letters *h* and *p* were used interchangeably.

A possible explanation for the striking similarity between the Hawaiian and Japanese syllabaries is that the ancient tribe of erstwhile Hawaiians may have migrated to the land of the Cherubim to escape the destruction of the Garden of Eden/ Mu continent/kingdom of Israel. As guests of the Cherubim, they would have remained there for a period of time until conditions on the earth returned to normal. This would have kept their language unchanged until their return to the region of their former homeland—finding only the present-day Hawaiian Islands, in which they settled. Perhaps modern Hawaiians who yearn to reconnect with their ancestors may do further research on this topic and voyage to the land of the Cherubim—Japan.

A very curious topographical feature in Hawaii may link it to the fabled Garden of Eden. Situated atop the southern end of the Waianae Mountain Range on the island of Oahu are the outlines of a male and female figure in repose along with a pyramid. This formation appears to be of natural origin; however, being linearly connected to one another and being of unquestionable gender— the male having features similar to statues on Easter Island, and the female as being with child—suggest a scene reminiscent of the Bible's Adam and Eve, the Garden of Eden, and the presence of divine Providence (the pyramid). The following photographs are of this very unusual natural formation.

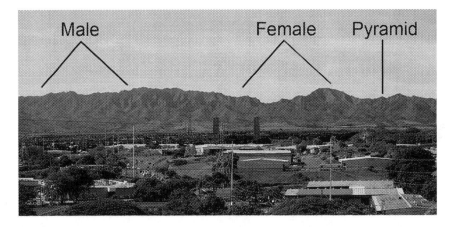

Male Formation

Female Formation

Pyramid viewed from the South. Satellite view reveals a pyramid with three sides. Google Earth: 21 25'54.99"N 158 05'25.29"W

Could these natural formations, being arranged in such a way by nature, be conveying a message of some kind? Perhaps, "This land is a remnant of the Garden of Eden"?

Anthropologists often use language to identify related cultures. Could the native Hawaiian culture be related to the culture of Japan? The Hawaiian culture and other native and aboriginal cultures of the Pacific Rim countries appear to share common ties and a common origin, and they were the established civilizations encountered by explorers during Europe's westward expansion. Could they have been the descendants of the lost kingdom of Israel/the lost Garden of Eden/the lost continent of Mu, and the lost tribes of Israel?

Various scriptures in the Bible lend credence to this possibility. Matthew 24:27 links the coming of the savior of Israel with a mysterious land in the east—"For as the lightning cometh out of the east, and shineth even unto the west; so shall also the coming of the Son of man be." "The lightning cometh out of the east" appears to be a reference to the mysterious land in the east from which the "light (of God) shines." "So shall also the coming of the Son of man be" indicates that the Son of man/ promised Messiah/Second Coming shall appear in that land. And Revelation 7:2-3 further links the promised Messiah with the land in the east: "And I saw another angel ascending from the east, having the seal of the living God." "Ascending" would indicate being born or raised in the land in the east.

Isaiah 41:25 helps identify the mysterious country in the East: "I have raised up one from the north, and he shall come; from the rising of the sun shall he call upon my name." That is, "from the rising of the sun"—the Land of the Rising Sun—identifies the country in the east from which the Son of man shall appear.

Other verses found in scripture link the country in the east from which the Messiah shall appear with the tribe of Judah. Genesis 49:10 identifies the tribe of Judah as the spiritual head ("scepter") of the house of Israel from which the Messiah ("lawgiver") shall appear: "The scepter shall not depart from

Judah, nor a lawgiver from between his feet, until Shiloh come; and unto him shall the gathering of the people be"—that is, the Messiah shall appear in the land in the east (the Land of the Rising Sun) where the tribe of Judah remains. Micah 5:2: "But thou, Bethlehem Ephratah, though thou be little among the thousands of Judah, yet out of thee shall he come forth unto me that is to be ruler in Israel" reveals that the promised Messiah/Son of man/Second Coming shall appear "among the thousands of Judah" in the Land of the Rising Sun, and he shall "be ruler in Israel" (i.e., "unto him shall the gathering of the people be").

These verse from scripture reveal the significance of the "land in the east," the Land of the Rising Sun. It would be safe to say that the destruction of the kingdom of Israel caused the dispersing of its people ("the lost tribes of Israel")—the tribe of Judah being established in "the land in the east"—the Land of the Rising Sun—"Zha Pan"—modern Japan.

There are also many verses in scripture that refer to God's restoration of the house of Israel in the latter days (e.g., Isaiah 2:2: "And it shall come to pass in the last days, that the mountain of the Lord's house shall be established in the top of the mountains . . . and all nations shall flow unto it"; Jeremiah 23:8: "The House of Israel . . . shall dwell in their own land"; and Ezekiel 34:23-28: "I will set up one shepherd over them, and he shall feed them, even my servant David . . . and I will make with them a covenant of peace . . . and the tree of the field shall yield her fruit, and the earth shall yield her increase, and they shall be safe in their land"). Do these prophecies coincide with the rise in the economies of Japan, China, and Korea?

Therefore, who are the lost sheep of the house of Israel? Perhaps the answer may be found in Genesis 28:14. In that verse, God reveals that the descendants of Jacob (Israel) "shall spread— as the dust of the earth—to the four corners of the earth and be a blessing to all the families of the earth." This revelation contains a vital spiritual meaning in addition to its significant literal meaning. *Spiritually speaking*, the revelation portends those with a spiritual relationship with ancient Israel would be born among the five colored races of mankind and serve as exemplars of righteous conduct and be a blessing to all the families of the earth. *Literally speaking*, would not the noble and exemplary conduct of the people of Japan during the devastating earthquake and tsunami of 2011 be an example of righteous conduct? Who are the lost sheep? The definitive answer is revealed when Christ said, "And ye shall know them by their works."

With the end of the fourth world age—the end of the Garden of Eden, the continent of Mu, and the ancient kingdom of Israel—the fifth world age would have its beginnings in the lands of Europe. There, the civilizations of the West would fulfill their mission to bring the world into the technological age of today.

Chapter 35

The Fifth World Age

The fourth world age of mankind ended with the destruction of the Garden of Eden and the kingdom of Israel. The Bible provides scant evidence—often in the form of vague references by patriarchs or prophets—for the emergence of a fifth world age. Genesis 27:39-40 refers to a future fifth world age with a characterization of the next civilization to have the dominion: "And Isaac his father answered and said unto him [unto Esau, Jacob's brother], Behold, thy dwelling shall be the fatness of the earth, and of the dew of heaven from above; and by thy sword shalt thou live, and shalt serve thy brother; and it shall come to pass when thou shalt have the dominion, that thou shalt break his yoke from off thy neck."

This is to say, "Thou shalt serve thy brother" meant that Esau would play a subordinate role during the fourth world age. "Thou shalt break his yoke from off thy neck" indicates that Esau would be given the dominant role in a future world age. "When thou shalt have the dominion" is to say that Esau would be the principal civilization during the fifth world age of man. "Thy dwelling shall be the fatness of the earth, and of the dew of heaven above" indicates that Esau would be those blessed with the ability to develop the material wealth of the earth. "And by thy sword shalt thou live" indicates that Esau would accomplish his God-given mission by the use of force or military might.

Luke 21:24 makes a reference to the "times of the Gentiles" (non-Israelites). This would be the time when the civilizations of the West would be given the leading role—"Thou shalt have the dominion"—to bring the world into the technological age of today. Thus, the fifth world age would have its beginnings in the lands of Europe with the ancient Greek civilization, succeeded by the Roman and other reigning empires of the West. Hence, Western history is said to have begun approximately five thousand years ago.

Scripture reveals that the world's previous four world ages all carried out their God-given missions and were retired. And so shall it be with the fifth world age of today. The book of Revelation encapsulates the history of the world since the time of its creation to the time of its demise at the end of the fifth world age. The Bible refers to the end of this fifth world age as the "End of the World."

Chapter 36

The End of the World

The literal translation of "world" is the "the age of man." Thus, "the end of the world" may be understood to mean the end of the age of man. The earth will continue to exist.

An example of an "end of the world" event may be found in the book of Genesis account of the great flood in the days of Noah. Scripture reveals that the earth had become corrupt before God with continual wickedness, evil, and violence. Thus, the earth was cleansed of all life by a great flood, except for Noah and his family, who had been given the mission to regenerate life anew.

Daniel 7:1-7 reveals that there would be four world ages of man: "Daniel spake and said, I saw in my visions by night, and, behold, the four winds of the heaven strove upon the great sea. And four great beasts came up from the sea, diverse one from another." The four great beasts represent four world ages of mankind.

These four world ages may be understood to be the ages of Noah, Abraham, Isaac, and Jacob. Thus, Noah, Abraham, Isaac, and Jacob are designated as patriarchs (fathers of the human race) that served as seed for new ages of mankind. The vision of the prophet Daniel does not speak of how each world age came to an end; however, the biblical account of the flood is a record of one of the endings of a world age. Although not stated, it may be understood that each of the four world ages of man was ended by cataclysms of nature. It would appear that the phenomenon of world ages mimics the cycle of life—birth, growth, maturity, decay, and death. Thus, it is common among world civilizations to say that their present civilization was preceded by an older, more advanced civilization often possessing high technology.

Hence, the Bible uses the analogy of God planting, nurturing, harvesting, and plowing asunder his garden in preparation for a new planting—that is, in preparation for a new world age. It is of interest that the ancient records of the Hopi Indians of North America, as presented in the *Book of the Hopi*, by Frank Waters, also record four world ages of man with each world age ending by various cataclysms of nature.

Science has determined that the earth has experienced at least five to more than twenty major mass extinctions of life on earth. Researcher Dr. Immanuel Velikovsky, through a series of books (*Earth in Upheaval*, *Worlds in Collision*, etc.) has presented geological evidence that mass extinctions of life on earth have been caused by cyclic, sudden, and violent physical upheavals of geologic change—the biblical flood being such an event.

Researcher Brent Miller of the Horizon Project has coordinated the latest scientific findings from the fields of astrophysics, physics, linguistics, archaeology, paleontology, ancient history, etc., that also validate the Bible's end-of-the-world revelations. Of interest are the fields of astronomy and astrophysics, which explain the cyclic route of the earth and its solar system throughout its Milky Way galaxy. Science has discovered that at the center of each galaxy lies a tremendous gravitational force called a "black hole," around which revolve a multitude of stars, including the sun. Due to the intense speed and gravitational force to which the planetary bodies are subjected, the galaxy assumes the shape of a flat disk, called the galactic plane. Viewed edgewise, the galaxy would appear similar to a phonograph record spinning around its galactic center. As our sun revolves around the galactic center, it travels above and below the galactic plane, completing this cycle every twenty-six thousand years. Thus, it is every thirteen thousand years that Earth's solar system passes through the galactic plane or "dark rift" (the collection of planetary bodies rotating around the edge of the galactic center/black hole). Passing through this "dark rift" is when the Earth is vulnerable to polar shifts, asteroid impacts, and severe climatic, solar, and geologic convulsions (i.e., the end of the world).

Through computer modeling, astrophysicists have determined that it takes approximately twenty years to pass through the galactic plane. Science estimates that our solar system will reach the midway point, the area where the earth will be subjected to the greatest disturbances, in the year 2012—more specifically, December 21, 2012. [Note that December 21, 2012—despite much controversy and fanfare—passed uneventfully prior to the completion of this book. Perhaps it was prophecy being fulfilled: "Hurt not the earth, neither the sea, nor the trees, till we have sealed the servants of our God in their foreheads" (Revelation 18:4).]

The year 2012 has also been correlated with what scholars have determined to be the end date of the ancient Mayan calendar. The Mayan calendar records astronomical and solar events that portend the ending of an age and, ostensibly, the beginning of a new age of man. This would be similar to the Bible's prophesy of the "end of the world" and the beginning of a thousand years of peace on earth. Thus, science provides compelling data that coincides with what has been prophesied by the ancient records of man found throughout the earth.

Of startling interest is science's search for the existence of a binary twin planet to the earth's sun. According to NASA, over 80 percent of all solar systems have multiple suns, and the search for the sun's binary twin has been well documented in the History Channel's *The Universe* series (season six, episode two: "Nemesis, the Sun's Evil Twin"). Referred to as "Nemesis," "Nibiru," "the Destroyer," "Planet X," etc., the orbit of this binary twin is believed to carry it into deep space and to return to earth's solar system every twenty-six million years. Stranger than fiction, the year 2012 has been deemed, through various harbinger events and computer modeling, to be the completion date for this twenty-six-million-year cycle.

Author, publisher, and lecturer Marshall Masters has provided groundbreaking data through his research and analysis of a broad range of scientific and ancient texts that support the existence and imminent return of the sun's binary twin planet (deemed to be a "brown dwarf" planet about the size of the planet Jupiter) on December 21, 2012. [Note that this date has been updated to late 2013 and early 2014.]

The significance in the return of this companion planet is that its orbit is projected to traverse the normal flow of the planets within our solar system. This will create great instability, and it may be what triggers the sun to begin its solar rampage "to scorch men with fire" as prophesied in scripture.

In the field of astronomy, an April 30, 2013, article by Space.com staff writer Miriam Kramer reports that astronomers are currently watching, with great interest, the appearance of comet C2012 S1 (ISON, named after the telescope responsible for its discovery). Referred to as the "comet of the century," comet ISON is unique because of its approach from the direction of the sun. It is projected to pass within 730,000 miles of the sun and the Earth in late November and December 2013, respectively. It will be eminently viewable with the possibility of appearing as bright as the moon. The close passage of Comet ISON may have the potential to trigger large solar flares that may seriously affect the earth.

For in-depth information on comet ISON, Dr. James M. McCanney has provided the latest, cutting-edge information on comets in an e-book, *Comets*, which devotes a whole chapter on the ramifications of comet ISON. Dr. McCanney expresses a concern that the passing of comet ISON through the solar system in January 2014 may precipitate events never seen before on earth. (The sudden appearance of comet ISON and the projected return of the sun's binary twin planet [*Nibiru*, Planet X, etc.] appear to be the same.)

There appears to be a confluence of data from religion and science concerning the end of the world. However, Matthew 24:36 provides a caution concerning the time of the end: "But of that day and hour knoweth no man, no, not the angels of heaven, but my Father only." And in this, neither religion nor science has put forward any date for when the world will come to an end.

In the book of Matthew, chapter 24, Jesus forewarns his disciples with several revelations concerning the time of the end: "And ye shall hear of wars and rumours of wars: see that ye be not troubled: for all these things must come to pass, but the end is not yet. For nation shall rise against nation, and kingdom against kingdom: and there shall be famines, and pestilences, and earthquakes, in divers places. All these are the beginnings of sorrows."

In the Second Epistle to Timothy, the apostle Paul continues with the words of Jesus: "This know also, that in the last days perilous times shall come. For men shall be lovers of their own selves, covetous, boasters, proud, blasphemers, disobedient to parents, unthankful, unholy, Without natural affection, trucebreakers, false accusers, incontinent, fierce, despisers of those that are good, Traitors, heady, highminded, lovers of pleasures more than lovers of God."

Jesus continues in the book of Matthew: "Now learn a parable of the fig tree: When his branch is yet tender, and putteth forth leaves, ye know that summer is nigh: So likewise ye, when ye shall see all these things, know that it is near, even at the doors. Verily I say unto you, This generation shall not pass, till all these things be fulfilled."

These revelations by Jesus and the apostle Paul appear to coincide with the present condition of the world and modern society. Thus, "When ye shall see all these things, know that it is near, even at the doors."

During the time of Noah and the flood, seed for the next world age was placed on a seagoing vessel (Noah's ark). In the present age of destruction by fire, scripture suggests that seed for the next world age may survive by being "taken" from the earth. This seems plausible because much time would be needed for the earth to recover from the great upheavals predicted in the Bible.

There are several references in the Bible concerning the sons of God, who have been intimately involved with humankind since the very beginning. The sons of God were involved with the creation of humankind—Genesis 1:26: "Let us make man in our image, after our likeness: and let them have dominion." The sons of God were involved with the appearance of superior human beings on earth—Genesis 6:1-4: "And it came to pass, when men began to multiply on the face of the earth, and daughters were born unto them, That the sons of God saw the daughters of men that they were fair; and they took them wives of all which they chose . . . and they bare children to them, the same became mighty men which were of old, men of renown." The sons of God were also involved with restraining humankind's bull-in-china-shop expansion—Genesis 11:1-8: "And the whole earth was of one language, and of one speech. And they (humankind) said, Go to, let us build us a city and a tower, whose top may reach unto heaven. And the Lord said, Behold, the people is one, and they have all one language; and this they begin to do: and now nothing will be restrained from them, which they have imagined to do. Go to, let us go down, and there confound their language, that they may not understand one another's speech."

These verses from the book of Genesis reveal that the sons of God were physical beings. They were human-like in appearance (man was made in their image and likeness), and they were able to take the daughters of men as wives and have children with them.

In Genesis 1:26, the sons of God said, "Let them have dominion." This suggests that the sons of God withdrew from the earth to allow man to rule it. Then, in Genesis 11:8, the Bible records them saying, "Let us go down." These verses suggest that the sons of God had the ability to leave the earth and return to it—most logically in flying craft.

Genesis 6:1-4 reveals that there were children born from the union of the sons of God and the daughters of men who became "mighty men which were of old, men of renown." It can be seen that these "men of renown" were half sons-of-God and half daughters-of-men lineage. It is reasonable to conclude that the "men of renown" also took wives and had children, who also had their own children and families. In such a way, the unique lineage of sons of God and daughters of men was carried forth by succeeding generations. This suggests the origin of the concept of a bloodline lineage.

There are traditions among native cultures that say their ancestors had contact with visitors from the stars. The Dogon, a primitive West African tribe, believe eons ago, their village was visited by human-like beings that came in a spaceship described to have three triangular legs. The visitors taught the Dogon ancestors the mysteries of creation and how to live. The Dogons have continued to carry on the knowledge of their ancient ancestors who, it is said, were taught by visitors from the constellation Sirius. The Dogon have advanced knowledge of our solar system, and they knew of the existence and location of a dwarf star called Sirius B, long before it was discovered by modern science.

In other parts of the world, the Japanese hold the belief that their ancestors came from the star cluster Pleiades. Native Americans also say that their ancestors came from the Pleiades and are awaiting their return. In Egypt, researchers Robert Bauval and Adrian Gilbert discovered that the alignment of the three main pyramids of Geza formed a pattern on the ground that was a mirror image of the three Belt Stars in the constellation of Orion. Also, researchers Virginia Trimble and Alexander Badawy have noted that shafts in the king's pyramid point toward the constellation of Orion. It is believed that the shafts would aid in the king's return to the stars of Orion. It is also interesting that the heavenly bodies Pleiades, Orion, Arcturus, and Mazzaroth should be mentioned in the Bible's book of Job.

Since the early forties, there have been increasing reports of sightings of extraterrestrial craft and documented accounts of people being "taken" aboard extraterrestrial vehicles. Some of those taken were shown the earth from space and then returned. Others were given foreknowledge concerning mankind's future should it continue on its present course.

Of related interest is an episode from the television series *Unsealed Alien Files*. In season 1, episode 13, "Aliens and Presidents," it was revealed that in 1777 at Valley Forge, Founding Father George Washington, then serving as commander in chief of the Continental Army, experienced contact with entities that some now consider to have been extraterrestrial beings. Seeking divine guidance during trying times at Valley Forge, George Washington witnessed a glowing spherical craft whose occupants revealed to him visions of America's future with cities expanding from coast to coast across North America. This suggested encouragement for George Washington to stay the course in America's war for independence. Thus, it would appear that the extraterrestrials were participants helping America to fulfill its role in the divine plan of God.

It has also often been revealed that the purpose for extraterrestrial contact is to help humankind prepare for the great upheavals that are to come. Perhaps these visitors are related to the Bible's sons of God returning to aid humankind during the end of the world prophesied in the Bible.

Scripture reveals that the world would first be cleansed of impurity through the use of fire (wars and economic and natural disasters), wind (great hurricanes, etc.) and water (tsunamis, storms, and floods). These events are referred to as the great tribulation/baptism of fire in which the "wheat (the pure) shall be separated from the chaff (the impure)." It will also be a period of salvation through baptism by Holy Spirit (Son of man). The promised Messiah and his disciples shall be offering salvation by transmitting the light of God through the palm of their hands just as was done nearly two thousand years ago during the time of Jesus.

In essence, "the end of the world" represents the end of the age in which God allowed mankind to follow the law of the jungle for the sake of material development of the earth. However, having fulfilled that part of God's divine plan, the earth and mankind are now experiencing the great transitional period of purification/tribulation in preparation for the new world age of righteousness and a thousand years of peace on earth.

Could science's extrapolation of December 21, 2012, as a date that portends dire consequences for all life on Earth actually be a revelation from God? That is, December 21, 2012, may serve as a juncture in scripture that signals the ending of the tribulation period and the beginning of sorrows.

Herewith is the book of Revelation's sequence of events— which are yet to come—heralding the end of the world:

1. Revelation 6:18: "And there was a great earthquake, such as was not since men were upon the earth, so mighty an earthquake, and so great." Note: Researchers and scientists have held quiet concern about increasing seismic activity along the New Madrid Fault in the Missouri region of the USA. According to St. Charles County Division of Emergency Management records, a magnitude 8+ quake that occurred along the New Madrid Fault in the year 1812 caused the Mississippi River to temporarily flow backward and change its course, and it also caused church bells to ring along the Eastern Seaboard. Of interest is a forecast made by remote viewer Major Ed Dames et al., who foresees an earthquake along the New Madrid Fault as being the next major catastrophic event of global significance. Could a major earthquake along the New Madrid Fault be related to the "great quake" in the book of Revelation?

2. Revelation 6:14-15: "And the heaven departed as a scroll when it is rolled together, and every mountain and island were moved out of their places. And the kings of the earth, and the great men, and the rich men, and every bondman, and every free man, hid themselves in the dens and in the rocks of the mountains."

3. Revelation 16:18-19: "And the great city was divided into three parts, and the cities of the nations fell, and great Babylon came in remembrance before God, to give unto her the cup of the wine of the fierceness of his wrath." Note that Revelation 17 and 18 describe that great city Babylon as "THE MOTHER OF HARLOTS AND ABOMINATIONS OF THE EARTH . . . which reigneth over the kings of the earth . . . for all nations have drunk of the wine of the wrath of her fornication, and the kings of the earth have committed fornication with her, and the merchants of the earth are waxed rich through the abundance of her delicacies." Could scripture be referring to a great financial capital of commerce and wealth akin to a Wall Street, with its golden calf? Scripture also forewarns the faithful, "And I heard another voice from heaven, saying, Come out of her my people, that ye be not partakers of her sins, and that ye receive not of her plagues" (Revelation 18:4).

4. Revelation 16:21: "And there fell upon men a great hail out of heaven, every stone about the weight of a talent: and men blasphemed God because of the plague of the hail; for the plague thereof was exceeding great." Note: The weight of a talent is estimated to be between sixty and 120 pounds. Hailstone of that size would be typical of the debris found in the tail of a comet. This suggests that the earth would be in the presence of a passing comet that could trigger the great quake of the earth and the onslaught of massive hailstones.

5. Revelation 18:8-20: "Therefore shall her plagues come in one day, death, and mourning, and famine, and she shall be utterly burned with fire for strong is the Lord God who judgeth her. And the kings of the earth, who have committed fornication and lived deliciously with her, shall bewail her, and lament for her, when they shall see the smoke of her burning. Standing afar off for the fear of her torment, saying, alas, alas, that great city Babylon that mighty city! For in one hour is thy judgment come. Rejoice over her, thou heaven, and ye holy apostles and prophets; for God hath avenged you on her."

6. Revelation 18:21: "And a mighty angel took up a stone like a great millstone, and cast it into the sea, saying, Thus with violence shall that great city Babylon be thrown down, and shall be found no more at all."

7. Revelation 19:9, 17, 20: "Blessed are they which are called unto the marriage supper of the Lamb . . . And I saw an angel standing in the sun; and he cried with a loud voice, saying to all the fowls that fly in the midst of heaven. Come and gather yourselves together unto the supper of the great God . . . And the beast was taken, and with him the false prophet that wrought miracles before him, with which he deceived them that had received the mark of the beast, and them that worshipped his image. These both were cast alive into a lake of fire burning with brimstone."

8. Revelation 20:2-3: "And he laid hold on the dragon, that old serpent, which is the Devil, and Satan, and bound him a thousand years. And cast him into the bottomless pit, and shut him up, and set a seal upon him, that he should deceive the nations no more, till the thousand years should be fulfilled: and after that he must be loosed a little season."

9. Revelation 20:4-6: "And I saw thrones, and they sat upon them, and judgment was given unto them: and I saw the souls of them that were beheaded for the witness of Jesus,

and for the word of God, and which had not worshipped the beast, neither his image, neither had received his mark upon their foreheads, or in their hands; and they lived and reigned with Christ a thousand years. But the rest of the dead lived not again until the thousand years were finished. This is the first resurrection. Blessed and holy is he that hath part in the first resurrection: on such the second death hath no power, but they shall be priests of God and of Christ, and shall reign with him a thousand years."

10. Revelation 20:7-10: "And when the thousand years are expired, Satan shall be loosed out of his prison, and shall go out to deceive the nations which are in the four quarters of the earth, Gog and Magog, to gather them together to battle: the number of whom is as the sand of the sea ... and fire came down from God out of heaven, and devoured them. And the devil that deceived them was cast into the lake of fire and brimstone, where the beast and the false prophet are, and shall be tormented day and night for ever and ever."

11. Revelation 20:11-15: "And I saw a great white throne, and him that sat on it ... And I saw the dead, small and great, stand before God; and the books were opened: and another book was opened, which is the book of life: and the dead were judged out of those things which were written in the books, according to their works. And the sea gave up the dead which were in it; and the dead were judged out of those things which were written in the books, according to their works. And death and hell were cast into the lake of fire. This is the second death. And whosoever was not found written in the book of life was cast into the lake of fire."

12. Revelation 21:1-4: "And I saw a new heaven and a new earth: for the first heaven and the first earth were passed away; and there was no more sea. And I John saw the holy city, new Jerusalem, coming down from God out of heaven, prepared as a bride adorned for her husband. And I heard a great voice out of heaven saying, Behold, the tabernacle of God is with men, and he will dwell with them, and they shall be his people, and God himself shall be with them, and be their God. And God shall wipe away all tears from their eyes; and there shall be no more death, neither sorrow, nor crying, neither shall there be any more pain: for the former things are passed away."

The book of Revelation suggests that the end of the present fifth world age would lead to a period of a thousand years of peace on earth in which the righteous would live with Christ in peace and harmony. After the thousand years of peace on earth, Satan would be set loose for a season to deceive the nations of the world, Gog and Magog, and to gather them to battle with the saints. Those nations would be devoured by fire from God out of heaven, and the devil that deceived them would be cast into the lake of fire forever and ever.

The day of judgment would then follow, and the books would be opened and all would be judged according to that which is written in those books, each according to his or her works. And death and hell and all those whose names were not found written in the book of life would be cast into the lake of fire. This would be the second death (eternal death?). Then John sees a new heaven and a new earth coming down from God in which the tabernacle of God will be with men, and this suggests an eternal heavenly existence.

Could the verses of scripture that portend what is yet to come for the world be too fantastic to be taken literally? The ancient monuments and megaliths of ancient civilizations that have long vanished from the earth suggest that the cycle of life is a reality that persists with indifference to the thoughts of men. Thus, our present world age shall certainly follow in the footsteps of previous world ages, and it too is fated to come to an end.

However, scripture suggests that this "end of the world" will not be the "final end." At the end of this present world age, scripture foretells that there shall follow a "thousand years of peace on earth," in which the meek and nonviolent shall inherit the earth and reign with Christ. Following this period of peace on earth, the world shall have another world age "for a season" that will culminate in the great battle between good and evil that has been popularly referred to as Armageddon. Scripture suggests that this shall be the "final end," in which there shall be judgment and erasing from the book of life (i.e., "the second death," in which the spiritual cells of souls shall be "erased" by being disbursed back into the universe from which they were originally derived).

A key point is that there is still time to become righteous, to become Christlike, and to return to being a child of God before the day of judgment. We all follow the cycle of life in which we travel between heaven and earth until we finally become Christlike in character. This is all done under the guidance and watchful eye of God. Therefore, there is absolutely nothing to fear when one is being watched over by God. Should God decide to call one back to heaven during this "end of the world" age, then one shall still have time to polish his or her soul and strive to become Christlike while in heaven. Scripture foretells the appearance of another world age in which one may choose to return to earth to continue the journey to grow spiritually. Is it not truly good news to know that it is not yet the "final end" and that there is still time to become Christlike?

God reveals in Revelation 21:7, "He that overcometh shall inherit all things; and I will be his God, and he shall be my son." This suggests that we are all being encouraged by God to strive to overcome our human imperfections and to become divine in character.

Despite scripture's dire forecast concerning conditions that will culminate in the "end of the world," the earth remains a place of immense beauty in which nature shines, and man's compassion for his fellow man is being displayed. Therefore, things are far from being all "doom and gloom." One should strive to maintain the heart of gratitude for everything from morning till night, to be a positive force for change in the world and for others.

Chapter 37

Prophecy

Bible prophecy is unique because it is attributed to the words of God, and it often concerns the affairs of man and its consequences. However, prophecy is often imparted in vague and uncertain terms when it would be more compelling if specific times and dates were given—albeit, those aspects of prophecy being strongly influenced by how man exercises "free will."

For example, the great flood in the days of Noah could have been avoided if not for man's continual evil and corruption of the earth and the way of God. Similarly, in Genesis 18:32, the Lord assured Abraham that if ten righteous people could be found in the city of Sodom, the city would not be destroyed for ten's sake. These revelations reveal three important points concerning prophecy:

1. Prophecy is not "written in stone." Prophecy often is an indicator of what will happen if things continue in a certain direction.
2. Man possesses the power to influence the outcome of prophecy by the choices that he makes—that is, man may choose to continue on a certain path and fulfill prophecy, or he may choose to reverse direction (repent) and thereby change the outcome.
3. God has the power to intervene and bestow divine protection. As examples, Revelation 9:4: "And it was

commanded them that they should not hurt the grass of the earth, neither any green thing, neither any tree; but only those men which have not the seal of God in their foreheads." Matthew 13:40: "So shall it be at the end of the world: the angels shall come forth, and sever the wicked from among the just." Matthew 25:32: "And before him shall be gathered all nations: and he shall separate them one from another, as a shepherd divideth his sheep [Children of God] from the goats [Man/beasts]."

Scripture reveals that only God knows when the end of the world will be (i.e., the exact time of the end is being determined by what man does). Thus, Jesus would say in Matthew 24:33, "So likewise ye, when ye shall see all these things, know that it is near, even at the doors." Do the "signs and seasons" indicate the fulfillment of prophecy in our modern age, and what might an individual do to make a difference concerning the "the end of the world"?

Those drawn to such concerns may be considered emissaries with the mission to save their families and loved ones by focusing on spiritual elevation. Serving in such a way may be likened to a single drop of rain that will be joined by many others to create a tremendous force for good in the world—surely to influence the outcome of that which has been prophesized for the end of the world. Therefore, it is important to view prophecy from a proactive perspective and become a "single drop of rain" working to save families and loved ones. This is an unprecedented opportunity to *directly* serve God by saving others, and it is a fortuitous opportunity to transform one's self into a child of God by helping to fulfill God's wish that all should not perish from the earth.

Chapter 38

What to Do

Scripture encourages "spiritual growth" with phrases such as, "Be thou perfect as your Father in Heaven is perfect" and "He that overcometh shall gain eternal life in Heaven."

To "Be thou perfect," and to "overcometh" mean to grow spiritually by eliminating human imperfections and shortcomings—such as greed, avarice, lust, hatred, violence, judging, resentment, and grudge, etc.—from one's character. Human imperfections and shortcomings are what cause separation from God, heaven, and good fortune.

The terms "Child of God," "man," and "beast" are mentioned in the Bible in reference to the various aspects of mankind. At the risk of oversimplification, it may be said:

- A "child of God" is one who follows the rules of society and the laws of God without being told to do so.
- A "man" is someone who may violate the rules of society or the laws of God but will refrain from doing so when corrected.
- A "beast" is someone who violates the rules of society or the laws of God, and will *not* correct his behavior when asked to do so.

These three characterizations or "spiritual levels" represent the unwritten task for each individual that has been granted life on earth: one should strive to elevate to the next level by making changes in one's way of thinking and in one's way of living (e.g., a change, among many, may be as simple as following the traffic laws or being courteous during a stressful situation, when it would not normally be done). Therefore, spiritual growth may be gained by gradually replacing the "way of the world" with ways that are more in tune with God's scriptural guidance—while maintaining the heart of *apology* (for one's shortcomings) and *gratitude* (for being able to correct them).

It should be noted that meditation is helpful to sharpen one's focus by clearing the mind of worldly distractions; however, true spiritual growth can only be attained through social interaction with others: God arranges others and situations to reveal one's hidden shortcomings; that is, the areas of one's character that must be refined and elevated.

As one progresses on the spiritual path and elevates in character, it can be said that one has left the "old self" and has emerged with a "new self" more divine in character. Such an achievement is what scripture refers to as "being reborn"—to which God may reply, "This is my child, of whom I am well pleased."

Life is filled with endless opportunities to grow spiritually by doing what is correct without being told to do so. Consider that God is watching with expectation.

An important role of parenting is to help children to grow spiritually by elevating to the next level—somewhat similar to teaching children to become responsible adults in a God-centered way. In this regard, it is important to know that parents and children usually share similar levels and that priority is always given to the parent because parents have been granted dominion over their children. Therefore, parents must "lead the way" in their own spiritual growth to successfully guide their children. A parent that is growing spiritually serves as the "rising tide that raises all boats."

Of equal importance are life's physical necessities. An end-time harbinger indicates that the world will experience "tribulation as a woman in travail" in preparation to receive a new heaven and earth. Thus, problem solving according to the old "way of the world" will become ineffective, resulting in deadlocks and impasses in all aspects of human endeavor. Therefore, being self-sufficient and informed about emergency preparedness will be very important. A common-sense approach and working within one's means are paramount. The following three basic areas should be considered:

- Water: supplies of water should be kept for emergencies. For the long term, an inexpensive gravity flow, ceramic water filter kit (Homespun Environmental) should be kept to filter water from lakes, streams, ponds, etc.
- Food: aside from supplies of food for emergencies, learning how to grow food by way of victory gardens, rooftop gardens, one-pot plantings, etc., should be a part of any preparedness plan.
- Knowledge of one's surroundings: knowing the advantages and disadvantages of one's environment and having an evacuation plan are also important.

Emergency preparedness is wise and necessary; however, emergency preparedness alone may not be enough to keep out of harm's way. It is spiritual growth that ultimately determines whether one may be at the right place at the right time to avoid disaster and misfortune. Therefore, spiritual growth should be the priority; hence, the Bible's eternal message is, "Repent!" That is, to place less priority on the "way of the world" (anything is permitted as long as it's "legal") and to begin living according to the way of God (following the laws of God).

Jesus's proclamation to "repent, the kingdom of heaven is at hand," was an admonishment to prepare for the imminent change in the divine plan of God. The way of God would replace the ruthless way of the world. Thus, the "end of the world" would be the long-awaited event that would return humankind to paradise. No longer would the world be a survival-of-the-fittest world. The law of the jungle (violence) would be replaced by the law of heaven; that is, the earth will be transformed into heaven on earth. The violent ways of the old earth shall all pass away: "The wolf and the lamb shall feed together, and the lion shall eat straw like the bullock" (Isaiah 65:25). Humankind would once more be of one brotherhood, in which people will "love thy neighbor as thyself," and everyone will "do unto others as ye would have others do unto you."

Therefore, it is imperative to begin to change one's way of thinking and doing things: change from the materialistic view to the spiritual view. Change from one who causes pollution to one who helps lessen pollution by reducing consumption, reusing materials, repairing items, and recycling items. Change from self-centeredness to one who is considerate of others. Become one who places priority on spiritual growth—striving to overcome human imperfections and shortcomings by incorporating "turn the other cheek," etc. (Matthew 5: 38-45), when being tested by God.

Become one who is able to discern right from wrong and leaves judging to God. Become one that can consider the physical body as something "on loan" from God—that is, being aware that one's body should be treated with respect and care by making effort to exercise and "feed" it the purest food within one's means, and allow nature (God/immune system) to work its miracles—doing so will be an expression of gratitude and acknowledgment to God.

Become one who practices neatness and tidiness and who goes about life in a calm and orderly fashion. Making effort will allow one to be closer to where sorrow and misfortune do not exist. Most importantly, and if one may receive it, seek the light of God—baptism by Holy Spirit/spiritual purification—to spiritually awaken and more quickly return to being a child of God.

The world should strive to greet "a new heaven and a new earth: for the first were passed away. Behold, the tabernacle of God is with men, and he will dwell with them, and they shall be his people, and God himself shall be with them, and be their God. And God shall wipe away all tears from their eyes; and there shall be no more death, neither sorrow, nor crying, neither shall there be any more pain: for the former things are passed away. He that overcometh shall inherit all things; and I will be his God, and he shall be my son" (Revelation 21:1-7).

*May God bless
and be with everyone.*

References

Ali, Abdullah Yusuf. *The Holy Qur'an*. Elmhurst, NY: Tahrike Tarsile Qur'an, 1987.

Amens, Daniel G., MD. *Change Your Brain, Change Your Life*. New York: Three Rivers Press, 1999.

Anderson, Johannes C. *Myths and Legends of the Polynesians*. Rutland, VT, and Tokyo: Charles E. Tuttle, 1986.

Anderson, Sir Norman, ed. *The World's Religions*. Grand Rapids, MI: William B. Eerdans, 1980.

Ballou, John. *Oahspe*. New York and London: Oahspe, 1882.

Bell, Fred Dr. *Rays of Truth—Crystals of Light*. Laguna Beach, CA: Pyradyne, 1999.

Berg, Dr. Philip S. *The Wheels of a Soul*. New York: Press of the Research Centre of Kabbalah, 1984.

Bergier, Jacques. *Extraterrestrial Visitations from Prehistoric Times to the Present*. Chicago: Henry Regnery, 1973.

Blavatsky, H. P. *The Secret Doctrine*. Wheaton, IL: Theosophical Publishing House, 1979.

Braghine, Colonel A. *The Shadow of Atlantis*. Kempton, IL: Adventures Unlimited Press, 1997.

Brown, John McMillan. *The Riddle of the Pacific*. Kempton, IL: Adventures Unlimited Press, 1996.

Budge, Wallis E. A. *The Egyptian Book of the Dead*. New York: Dover Publications, 1967.

Bukkyo Dendo Kyokai. *The Teaching of Buddha*. Tokyo: Kosaido Printing, 1966.

Cannon, Dolores. "Lost Knowledge and Aliens," interview by George Noory, Coast-to-Coast AM, April 04, 2013. http://www.coasttocoastam.com/show/2013/04/04.

Carter, Howard. *The Tomb of Tutankhamen*. New York: Excalibur Books, E. P. Dutton, USA, 1954.

Cayce, Hugh Lynn. *The Edgar Cayce Collection*. New York: Bonanza Books, 1969.

Childress, David Hatcher. *Lost Cities of Ancient Lemuria and The Pacific*. Kempton, IL: Adventures Unlimited Press, 1988.

Churchward, James. *The Children of Mu*. Albuquerque, NM: BE Books, 1988.

—. *The Cosmic Forces of Mu*. New York: Paperback Library, 1970.

—. *The Lost Continent of Mu*. Albuquerque, NM: BE Books, 1987.

—. *The Sacred Symbols of Mu*. Albuquerque, NM: BE Books, 1988.

Cotterell, Maurice. *Future Science*. West Cork, Ireland: Celtic Press, 2011.

Crim, Keith, ed. *The Perennial Dictionary of World Religions*. San Francisco: Harper & Row, 1981.

Davis, Albert Roy, and Walter C. Rawls, JR. *The Magnetic Blueprint of Life*. Kansas City, MO: Acres, 1993.

Dykstra, Andrew. *The Kanji ABC*. Honolulu: Kanji Press, 1987.

Edwards, I. E. S. *Treasures of Tutankhamun*. New York: Ballantine Books, 1976.

Essene, Virginia, and Sheldon Nidle. *You Are Becoming a Galactic Human*. Santa Clara, CA: Spiritual Endeavors, 1995.

Goi, Masahisa. *God and Man*. Chiba, Japan: Byakko Press, 1983.

Hatcher, William S., and J. Douglas Martin. *The Baha'i Faith*. San Francisco: Harper and Row, 1985.

The Holy Bible. Catholic Version. Chicago: Catholic Press, 1960.

The Holy Bible. Authorized King James Version. Grand Rapids, MI: Zondervan Bible Publishers, 1962.

Joseph, Frank. *The Lost Civilization of Lemuria*. Rochester, VT: Bear, 2006.

Judd, Henry P. *Introduction to the Hawaiian Language*. Honolulu: Tongg, 1971.

Kaibara, Ekiken. *Yojokun Japanese Secret of Good Health*. Tokyo: Tokuma Shoten, 1974.

Kirimura, Yasuji. *Fundamentals of Buddhism*. Santa Monica, CA: World Tribune Press, 1982.

LitCouture. 2012. http://www.englishmajorsunite.com.

Long, Max Freedom. *The Secret Science behind Miracles*. Marina Del Ray, CA: DeVorrs, 1976.

Maclean, Charles. *The Wolf Children*. New York: Hill and Wang, 1977.

Marciniak, Barbara. *Bringers of the Dawn*. Santa Fe, NM: Bear, 1992.

Masters, Marshall. "Coming Cataclysms," interview by George Noory, Coast-to-Coast AM, April 30, 2012. http://www.coasttocoastam.com/show/2012/04/30.

McCanney, James. "Comet ISON," interview by George Noory, Coast-to-Coast AM, January 14, 2013. http://www.coasttocoastam.com/show/2013/01/14.

McCrone, John. *The Myth of Irrationality*. New York: Carroll and Graf, 1994.

Metzger, Bruce M., ed. *The Reader's Digest Bible*. Pleasantville, NY: Reader's Digest Association, 1982.

Miller, Brent. "Coming Pole Shift," interview by George Knapp, Coast-to-Coast AM, January 11, 2009. http://www.coasttocoastam.com/show/2009/01/11.

Nichiren Shoshu International Center. *Lectures on the Sutra*. Tokyo, 1978.

Nishiyama, Teruo. *Introduction to the Teachings of Tenrikyo*. Nara, Japan: Tenri Jihosha, 1981.

Oda, James. *The Jewish and Alien Heritage of Ancient Japan*. Self-published, Northridge, CA, 1997.

Okawa, Ryuho. *The Laws of the Sun*. Tokyo: IRH Press, 1991.

Pye, Lloyd. "Intervention Theory," interview by George Noory, Coast-to-Coast AM, December 13, 2005. http://www.coasttocoastam.com/show/2005/12/13.

Robbins, John. *Diet for a New America*. Walpole, NH: Stillpoint, 1987.

Senior, Donald. *The Catholic Study Bible*. New York: Oxford University Press, 1990.

Shillony, Ben-Ami. *The Jews and the Japanese*. Rutland, VT, and Tokyo: Charles E. Tuttle, 1991.

Singh, Joseph Amrito Lal. "Diary of the Wolf-Children of Midnapore," http//www.midnapore.in/wolf-children-of-midnapore1.html (accessed August 2013).

Sitchin, Zecharia. *The Stairway to Heaven*. New York: St. Martin's Press, 1980.

Smith, Jeff. "GMO Health Danger," interview by George Noory, Coast-to-Coast AM, September 12, 2012. http://www.coasttocoastam.com/show/2012/09/12.

Smith, Joseph. *The Book of Mormon*. Salt Lake City, UT: Church of Jesus Christ of Latter-day Saints, 1981.

Sparks, Jim. *The Keepers*. Columbus, NC: Wild Flower Press, 2006.

Stearn, Jess. *Edgar Cayce—The Sleeping Prophet*. Garden City, NY: Doubleday, 1967.

Tebecis, Andris K., PhD. *Mahikari Thank God for the Answers at Last*. Tokyo: L. H. Yoko Shuppan, 1982.

Tensho-Kotai-Jingu-Kyo. *Divine Manifestations*. Tabuse, Yamaguchi Pref., Japan, 1970.

—. *The Prophet of Tabuse*. Tabuse, Yamaguchi Pref., Japan, 1954.

Tsarion, Michael. *Atlantis Alien Visitation and Genetic Manipulation*. Santa Clara, CA: Angels at Work, 2004.

Velikovsky, Immanuel. *Earth in Upheaval*. New York: Dell, 1955.

—. *Worlds in Collision*. New York: Doubleday, 1950.

Von Daniken, Erick. *Chariots of the Gods*. New York: Berkley Books, 1968.

—. *Gods from Outer Space*. New York: Bantam Books, 1968.

Waters, Frank. *Book of the Hopi*. New York: Penguin Books, 1977.

Wilcock, David. *The Source Field Investigations*. New York: Dutton, 2011.

Williams, George M. *NSA Seminars: An Introduction to Buddhism*. Santa Monica, CA: World Tribune Press, 1982.

Wilson, Colin, and Rand Flem-Ath. *The Atlantis Blueprint*. New York: Delacorte Press, 2001.

Winter, Ruth. *A Consumer's Dictionary of Food Additives*. New York: Crown Publishers, 1989.

Wright, Ted. *Wright's Complete Disaster Survival Manual*. Charlottesville, VA: Hampton Roads, 1993.